The
—— EVA——
Challenge

Advance Comments on *The EVA Challenge*

"Moving beyond describing the financial calculation of EVA and EVA-based bonus schemes, Stern and Shiely build an integrated approach to managing complex organizations in dynamic environments. Spanning recent research in strategy, management, accounting, finance, and economics, they offer a comprehensive framework of corporate governance—getting managers to act in shareholders' interest."

> —Jerold Zimmerman, Ronald L. Bittner Professor, Simon School, University of Rochester

"There is nothing more practical than a good theory. The ideas developed in this book rest on the seminal contributions of two Nobel laureates, Merton Miller and Franco Modigliani, and their subsequent Chicago students such as Fama, Scholes, Jensen, and Joel Stern himself. I found this book very practical in developing a firm's value creation strategy that benefits all stakeholders regardless of market considerations."

> —Robert S. Hamada, Dean and Edward Eagle Brown Distinguished Service Professor of Finance

"Stern and Shiely have produced a winner. The EVA Challenge not only serves as a useful how-to guide, but an important road map for anyone implementing a performance system that will ultimately provide value creation for the shareholder."

> —C. B. Rogers, Jr., former Chairman and Chief Executive Officer, Equifax

"*The EVA Challenge* is a path-breaking book, lucidly written, which reveals the underlying economic reality of a firm, the way to measure the true profit and loss."

> —Daniel Bell, Henry Ford II Professor of Social Sciences, Harvard University, Emeritus

"A firm's success depends crucially on its ability to monitor the performance of its management team and to reward them correspondingly. Managers who want to understand how EVA is helping firms to tackle these twin problems cannot do better than to read *The EVA Challenge.*"

> —Richard Brealey, Visiting Professor of Finance, London Business School

"Joel Stern has played a crucial role in advancing our knowledge of how to design company performance and managerial compensation schemes. . . . it is grounded in a strong intellectual framework that economists can recognize. . . . a readable and hands-on-approach. . . . [that] will interest both practitioners and students of finance."

> —Julian Franks, Professor of Finance, London Business School

"As Joel Stern and John Shiely vividly demonstrate, the real key to success with EVA is providing EVA training and incentives at all levels in the organization. At SPX, where virtually every one of our employees is on an EVA bonus plan, the system has helped us achieve breakthroughs in efficiency and profitability that few people thought possible."

> —John B. Blystone, Chairman, President, and CEO, SPX Corporation

"To be sure, this book is an indispensable guide for any organization considering a move to EVA. But it's also a highly readable primer for anyone who simply wants to learn more about what EVA can mean for companies, their shareholders and stakeholders."

> —James D. Ericson, Chairman and Chief Executive Officer, Northwestern Mutual

The EVA Challenge

Implementing Value-Added Change in an Organization

By Joel M. Stern and John S. Shiely,
with Irwin Ross

John Wiley & Sons, Inc.

New York • Chichester • Weinheim • Brisbane • Singapore • Toronto

Copyright © 2001 by Joel M. Stern and John S. Shiely. All rights reserved.

Published by John Wiley & Sons, Inc.
Published simultaneously in Canada.

This publication is designed to provide accurate and authoritative information in regard to the subject matter covered. It is sold with the understanding that the publisher is not engaged in rendering professional services. If professional advice or other expert assistance is required, the services of a competent professional person should be sought.

EVA® is a registered trademark of Stern Stewart & Co.

Library of Congress Cataloging-in-Publication Data:

Stern, Joel M.
    The EVA challenge : implementing value added change in an organization / by Joel M. Stern and John S. Shiely with Irwin Ross.
        p.   cm. — (Wiley finance)
    ISBN 0-471-40555-8 (cloth: alk. paper)
    1. Economic value added.   I. Shiely, John S.   II. Ross, Irwin
III. Title.   IV. Wiley finance series.

HG4028.V3 S83   2001
658.15—dc21   00-047993

Printed in the United States of America.

10 9 8 7 6 5 4 3 2 1

Contents

Chapter 1

The Problem

Back in the early 1960s, one of the authors of this volume was asked by an old family friend what he was studying at the University of Chicago. "I'm trying to come up with what determines the value of a company," said the young Joel Stern. "Even like my store?" asked the old friend, who ran a mom-and-pop grocery store. "Of course." The grocer was incredulous: "You're going to school for that! Come down to the store tomorrow and I'll show you what determines the value of a company." The next morning, he escorted a skeptical Joel behind the counter and pointed to a cigar box. "This is where we put the money," he explained. "If the lid is rising during the day, it means we're doing fine."

This simple insight into the basic importance of cash in valuing a business has always been known by the entrepreneur. Indeed, he can often work it out on the back of an envelope, comparing his total expected return with what he could plausibly earn elsewhere with the same amount of money at the same level of risk—in other words, the opportunity cost of capital. What has befogged this insight and prevented most investors from making these calculations has been two major developments in American capitalism: (1) the split between ownership and control of publicly held corporations and (2) the widespread acceptance of accounting measurements to gauge corporate value, a purpose for which they were never intended.

To start with the first point: the essence of the problem is that although numerous shareholders own a public corporation, control over its operations is in the hands of professional managers, who typically hold relatively few shares and whose interests often diverge from those of the silent majority of shareholders. Moreover, the managers possess detailed information about the company's prospects that outside shareholders lack, despite the best efforts of security analysts to inform them.

The divorce between ownership and control had been going on for a long time, and was by no means a secret when, in 1932, the subject was explored in depth in a blockbuster book, *The Modern Corporation and Private Property*, by two Columbia University professors, Adolf A. Berle Jr. and Gardiner C. Means. The authors chronicled the growth of the modern corporation in the United States from its start in the late eighteenth century, when companies built bridges, canals, and turnpikes. Early in the next century came the extension of the corporate form to the textile industry, its later dominance of the railroad industry and, afterward, of oil, mining, telephone, steel, and almost every other industry.

Berle and Means boldly asserted, in 1932, that so powerful were the large corporations that "private initiative" was now nonexistent, that self-perpetuating groups of managers dominated the economy and often pursued agendas contrary to the interests of owners and, presumably, to that of the country as a whole. Their rhetoric at times seems excessive, and may well have been influenced by the book's publication in the depths of the Great Depression. Timing may also have heightened the impact of the book, but its renown has extended over the decades, and it is still in print.

It is a book worth recalling, for it foreshadows the present concern with "corporate governance"—a high-flown term for a search for systems to get managers to act in the interests of shareholders. For a given degree of risk, shareholders obviously seek the highest total return—the sum of dividend payments plus share price appreciation. Managers, by contrast, often tend to be preoccupied by their personal pecuniary interests. The book's examples of conflicts of interest between managers and shareholders are both hair-raising and anachronistic—and are doubtless evidence that things have improved since 1932. Thus, it gives many examples of self-dealing, with managers typically funneling purchases to suppliers that they covertly own, as well as various types of fraud that have become less common in the years since that powerful police agency, the Securities and Exchange Commission (SEC), was established in 1934. The book also mentions a form of managerial imprudence not unknown today: the pursuit of growth for its own sake, to enhance the prestige and personal net worth of top executives, even when that growth is uneconomic and diminishes shareholder value.

Lacking the inside information of the managers, shareholders today, as in 1932, attempt to monitor their companies' performance using presumably objective criteria—the measures that accountants use. The difficulty is that the criteria are inadequate and downright misleading, however, much hallowed by tradition. What they do not necessarily reveal is the rising or declining level of the cash in the cigar box. Thus, net income—the so-called bottom line, which in turn is translated into earnings per share (EPS)—has long been elevated to supreme importance, not to say deified by most security analysts and the financial press. As a company's EPS grows, its share price is supposed to rise, on the assumption that its price/earnings (P/E) ratio remains relatively constant. There is an agreeable simplicity to this shorthand valuation, but it is as fallacious as it is ubiquitous.

To work their way to the bottom line, accountants make several calculations on a company's profit-and-loss statement that distort economic reality. The distortions err on the conservative side, thereby understating the true value of the enterprise. For example, since 1975, standard accounting procedure has been to "expense" research and development (R&D) outlays—that is, deduct them from revenues in the year in which the disbursements are made, even though the impact of such R&D is likely to be beneficial for many years in the future. The alternative would be to regard R&D as an investment and "capitalize" it—that is, put it on the balance sheet as an asset and write it off gradually over its expected useful life. The effect of expensing R&D is to understate the company's true profit for the year (and also, of course, lower its tax bill). In this case, both Generally Accepted Accounting Principles (GAAP) and the law leave no choice to the accountant. The degree of distortion varies, naturally, from company to company. Some may have little or no R&D, whereas it is a big cost item in high-tech companies and in pharmaceutical houses, which spend billions searching for new drugs. These companies are generally worth a great deal more in economic terms than their EPS indicates.

Advertising and marketing costs are also deducted in the year incurred. At first blush, this practice looks sensible inasmuch as the impact of advertising seems evanescent. In some cases it is, but advertising and marketing dollars often have a long-term impact in building brand value. With many consumer products, from bottled drinks to breakfast foods, advertising alone has produced scores of household names over the past half century. Logically, these costs should be capitalized and then written down over their expected useful lives. The same reasoning applies to the costs of training personnel—a particularly large item in the banking and insurance industries.

Accounting practice similarly causes distortion on a company's balance sheet. An asset is listed either at original cost, less depreciation, or at market value—whichever is lower. In a rising market, this obviously understates value. You've paid $10 million for a building, but it is now worth $20 million. You carry it on the balance sheet at $9 million. In economic terms, it hardly makes sense.

When one company buys another, there have been, for decades, two ways of handling the purchase. In a "pooling of interest" transaction, with payment made in the stock of the buying company for the shares of the target, the assets of the two entities are simply merged on the balance sheet, with no purchase premium recorded on the buyer's balance sheet, which means no adverse impact on future earnings. But in a purchase for cash (or some combination of cash and securities), different rules have applied. If the purchase price is greater than the "fair" asset value of the company being bought, the excess has to be treated as "goodwill" on the balance sheet of the merged company. It is then amortized over a period not to exceed 40 years, with the result that net income is less each year than it would otherwise be. But note that, in terms of economic reality, nothing has changed. Once there were two companies; now there is one. With a "purchase" procedure, earnings are depressed; but in a "pooling," there is no effect whatsoever. After years of criticism, serious moves are underway to outlaw pooling.

Accountants, however, are not intentionally perverse. Their focus is simply not on criteria relevant to shareholders—measurements that assess the underlying economic reality of the company. Rather, the accountants' historic purpose is to value assets and the operating condition of the company conservatively, to determine residual value under the worst circumstances. Essentially, their labors are designed to protect a corporation's bondholders and other lenders, to give them a sense of what they could collect if the company went belly-up. Jerold Zimmerman, professor of accounting at the University of Rochester's Simon School of Business, gave a succinct account of the rationale behind corporate accounting at a Stern Stewart roundtable discussion in 1993 that later appeared in the Summer 1993 issue of the *Journal of Applied Corporate Finance:*

> "The problem that the accounting and auditing systems were origi- nally designed to solve was the very basic problem of stewardship"— that is, were the company's employees using its money and other assets for the company's or their own purposes? "Another important function . . . was to control conflicts of interest between a com- pany's bondholders and its shareholders. The problem was this: how could managers, as representatives of the shareholders, make credible promises to the bondholders that they would not pay out excessively high dividends or invest in excessively risky projects? To reduce these conflicts, companies contracted privately with their bondholders to hire reputable, third-party accounting firms to gather and report certain kinds of information that would be useful in monitoring management's compliance with debt covenants."

This went on for many years. Soon after the SEC was created, it mandated the periodic publication of these accounting measure- ments in the interest of full disclosure to market participants. The calculations thus became the standard reporting tools in annual and quarterly reports and in news stories. They are mostly useful to the lenders. As Zimmerman pointed out, "Lenders care primarily only about downside risk. Lenders are much less interested than shareholders in going-concern values, and much more concerned about liquidation values. They want to know what the assets will be worth if the company can't meet its interest payments." The ac- countants provide that information, but they reveal little about shareholder value. Simply put, a shareholder wants to compare the cash he can take out of a company with the cash he invested. The cash he can take out is represented by the company's market value, not the accountant's book value.

Through long usage, however, earnings per share have come to dominate the headlines when a company issues its quarterly and an- nual reports. Tradition and ingrained habits are difficult to shake.

Not only does EPS distort reality, but the calculation is also easily manipulated by senior executives whose bonuses may be tied to earnings improvement. One way to produce a quick fix is to cut back on R&D or advertising, in order to lower costs and thus raise stated profits.

Another trick often employed in consumer goods companies is to force-feed compliant customers. It is known as "trade loading." Before the end of an accounting period, customers are persuaded to accept more merchandise than they need, and are given extended credit so they won't be billed until many months later. The sales are recorded when the goods are shipped—typically, just before the end of an accounting period, either a quarter or the fiscal year. Both sides ostensibly benefit: the manufacturer through an inflated EPS, and the customer through generous credit terms. But clearly it is a shell game, of no economic value to the company and of help only to executives whose incentive compensation is tied to EPS or whose stock options may be more valuable if a boost in EPS lifts the company's share price (a result that can occur because the market is ignorant of what prompted the rise in EPS). The next year, of course, the force-feeding has to be greater, lest sales decline—unless, of course, there is a real increase in sales.

For years, Quaker Oats indulged in that game until finally ending it in the early 1990s. As its former CEO, William Smithburg, said at another Stern Stewart roundtable, "Trade loading is an industry-wide practice that creates large artificial peaks and valleys in demand for our products [that] in turn generate significant extra infrastructure and extra inventory costs—all things you really would like to get rid of." Quaker Oats finally did so. "While this change did cause a temporary decline in our quarterly earnings, it clearly increased the economic value of our operations," Smithburg added.

In a widely heralded speech in September 1998, SEC chairman Arthur Levitt Jr., listed several other gimmicks involved in "earnings management." One was the "big bath" of restructuring charges— overstating the expenses of restructuring, which includes such things as severance payments for laid-off workers and the costs of shutting down facilities. "Why are companies tempted to overstate these charges?" he asked. "When earnings take a major hit, the theory goes [that] Wall Street will look beyond a one-time loss and focus only on future earnings and if these charges are conservatively estimated with a little extra cushioning, that so-called conservative estimate is miraculously reborn as income when estimates change or future earnings fall short."

A second gimmick is what Levitt called "merger magic" when a company merges with or acquires another company. One of the tricks is to call a large part of the acquisition price "'in process' research and development." This enables it to be written off immediately, so as not to be part of the "good will" on the balance sheet that would depress future earnings. "Equally troubling is the creation of large liabilities for future operating expenses to protect future earnings—all under the mask of an acquisition." When the liabilities prove to be exaggerated, they are reestimated and—presto!—converted into profit.

Companies that have not made an acquisition use a similar tactic that Levitt called "cookie jar reserves." It also involves bookkeeping sleight of hand by "using unrealistic assumptions to estimate liabilities for such items as sales returns, loan losses, or warranty costs. In doing so, they stash accruals in cookie jars during the good times and reach into them when needed in the bad times." Levitt gave an example of "one U.S. company who [sic] took a large one-time loss to earnings to reimburse franchisees for equipment. That equipment, however, which included literally the kitchen sink, had yet to be bought. And, at the same time, they announced that future earnings would grow an impressive 15 percent a year."

Levitt has not been alone in decrying such practices. In March 1999, Warren Buffett made headlines with an unexpected attack on top-ranking executives who delude investors. In the annual report of Berkshire Hathaway, his fabulously successful investment vehicle, Buffett stated, "Many major companies still play things straight, but a

significant and growing number of otherwise high-grade managers—
CEOs you would be happy to have as spouses for your children or
trustees under your will—have come to the view that it's okay to manipulate earnings to satisfy what they believe are Wall Street's de-
sires. Indeed, many CEOs think this kind of manipulation is not only
okay, but actually their *duty*." He praised Levitt's campaign to curb
the abuses.

It will be difficult, however, to end this gimmickry as long as so
many companies tie executive bonuses, in whole or in part, to improvements in EPS. The problem with that linkage, however, has
long been recognized. A number of corporate compensation committees have sought to escape the EPS trap by basing bonuses, at
least in part, on different earnings-based measurements such as return on equity (ROE), return on investment (ROI), or return on
net assets (RONA). These are better indicators of corporate performance because they include the balance sheet, but they all share a
basic flaw: they too can be manipulated. If return on equity is the
target, there are two ways to improve it. One is by better corporate
performance over time. But if that is not possible, there is another
strategy: reduce the equity in the company by buying-in shares,
either with cash on hand or with debt to finance the repurchase.
With fewer shares outstanding, and the same level of profit, the return on equity obviously rises. The executive suite is well served,
but not necessarily the shareholders.

If the bonus is linked to return on net assets, the same kind of
manipulation is possible. Some assets might be sold, even though
they might be worth more if kept, if their loss does not proportion-
ally reduce the profitability of the enterprise. The result will be
a higher return on the remaining assets. If this tack is not taken, a
bonus dependent on RONA can still be insidious by discouraging
profitable future growth. A promising acquisition, for example,
might not be made because the effect would be to lower the return
on assets by increasing the asset base, even though the total profitability of the enterprise would be enhanced.

Bonuses aside, there is another problem with current compensation schemes: executive compensation increases with the size of the enterprise. This is almost a law of nature and seems eminently logical. A larger empire means enlarged responsibilities for the top executives, presumably requiring greater talent and more impressive leadership qualities, and thus deserving of higher rewards. But growth and enhanced shareholder value are not the same thing; the system sets up a perverse incentive: corporate growth for the sake of the personal rewards it brings. As previously mentioned, Berle and Means noted this phenomenon back in 1932 and attributed the motive to the prestige that accrued to top executives. There is certainly prestige a-plenty in robust expansion, but more palpable is the larger pay packet that the CEO, the CFO, and the COO all receive. And the easiest way to expand is to merge and acquire—or "engulf and devour," as that wildly funny film, *Silent Movie*, with Sid Caesar, put it some years ago.

In the 1960s and 1970s, the urge to expand took a new form. In the past, companies on an acquisition binge sought to buy out their rivals, though there were always some that strayed into alien territory. But in the mid-1960s the drive to diversify became something of a mass phenomenon. It had a new name—the conglomerate—and a new rationale. In the past, there had been a sense that a corporation had best stick to its knitting or, as we now say, its core competencies. Suddenly, analysts and commentators began to herald the virtues of diversification. By buying companies in unrelated fields, the conglomerate managers could produce a steady earnings stream by offsetting cyclical declines in one industry with upswings in another. Strong financial controls radiating from the center would impose discipline and generate efficiencies in subordinate units without micromanaging them. Such at least was the theory, but reality did not bear it out.

The new conglomerate leaders—Harold Geneen of ITT, Charles Bludhorn of Gulf + Western, James J. Ling of Ling-Temko-Vought—became household names. Geneen, the subject of endless admiring articles in the financial press, gobbled up around 350 companies around the world—from hotel chains to telecommunications to a lone book publisher in New York. While the fad was on, the highly touted conglomerates enjoyed a run-up in their share prices, but there were few long-distance runners.

Many of the acquisitions were disasters, such as Mobil's purchase of Montgomery Ward and Ling-Temko-Vought's purchase of the Jones & Laughlin steel company when that industry had already embarked on its long decline. Although some well-run conglomerates have been successful—General Electric is always mentioned—the conglomerates basically failed because their organizational form did not add any value to the disparate entities under the corporate umbrella. Neither significant economies of scale nor productive efficiencies were realized. Each conglomerate provided a diversified portfolio for its investors, but at a considerable and unnecessary premium. Investors seeking diversification could more cheaply pick their own portfolios, or buy mutual funds.

By the late 1970s, widespread disillusion with conglomerates led to a lot of talk about true value and the rise of both the hostile takeover artists—Carl Icahn, Irwin Jacobs, Sir James Goldsmith, T. Boone Pickens—and the leveraged buyout movement. The so-called raiders sought out companies that appeared undervalued. They silently bought up shares until they reached a threshold percentage, at which point the law compelled them to make a public declaration of intent. Thereafter, they would approach the target company with an offer to buy, be rebuffed as expected, and then launch a tender offer to shareholders at a price significantly above where the stock was trading. The raiders talked much about shareholder value and how it had been betrayed by incumbent management. They often spoke the truth, but their ardor as the shareholders' friend was often brought into question by their willingness to sell their own shares to the target company at a substantial profit—an exercise that came to be called greenmail. Cynics suggested that the pursuit of greenmail was the sole motive involved, though in many cases the hostile bid succeeded and the outsiders became managers. (Icahn, for example, ran TWA for some years.) But their main contribution, beyond question, was to focus attention on how shareholder value had been squandered.

The leveraged buyout (LBO) phenomenon was far more significant. It also arose from the availability of companies performing below their potential, with their share prices reflecting their dismal record. Such companies had long been sought by entrepreneurs looking for turnaround situations, but what was unique about LBOs was the way they were financed. In a deft bit of fiscal legerdemain, the purchaser raised most of the money by hocking the assets and cash flow of the target company, investing relatively little equity. It was much like the process of buying a house, with the buyer making a cash down payment, and getting a mortgage loan, with the house as collateral. The difference is that, in an LBO, the loan is paid down not by the personal income of the buyer but by the future cash flow of the business, as well as by sales of underperforming assets.

The origins of LBOs can be traced back to the early 1960s, though they were initially quite small and not known by that name; "bootstrap financing" was the term most commonly used. Jerome Kohlberg Jr., then at Bear Stearns, did his first leveraged buyout of a small company in 1965. An insurance company provided the necessary loan. The following year, the company went public and Kohlberg soon had a personal profit of $175,000. Everybody in the deal made money.

Other bootstrap operations followed, with Kohlberg now assisted by two cousins, Henry Kravis and George Roberts. In 1976, the trio resigned from Bear Stearns and formed Kohlberg, Kravis and Roberts (KKR). They didn't make much of a stir at first, but by 1983 they were dominating the flourishing LBO business. Their deals ranged from $420 million to over $800 million. Those seemed like big numbers at the time, but multibillion-dollar deals were to follow within a few years. Forstmann Little was KKR's biggest competitor, and there were several other rivals in the field.

Until the advent of junk bonds, the deals were financed by revolving bank loans, conventional bonds and debentures, preferred stock bought by insurance companies and other institutions, and equity pools raised from public pension funds and private investors. When junk bonds became available in the mid-1980s, much bigger deals became possible. KKR raised its first billion-dollar equity fund in 1984. It was not actually a fund that sat idle waiting for deals, but a commitment that could be drawn down at any time. The debt-to-equity ratio in a buyout typically ranged from 4-to-1 to as high as 8-to-1. KKR was the general partner in every deal, with its equity investors having the legal status of limited partners. Its rewards were generous. It received an investment banking fee of about 1 percent for cobbling the deal together, which it generally took in the form of stock in the new company, annual consultant fees for the companies in its portfolios, a fee of 1.5 percent a year on the money in its equity pool and—the big kicker—20 percent of the profit the equity partners made. KKR representatives sat on the board of every company they controlled.

In the typical deal, KKR would retain the incumbent managers after taking the company private and would arrange for them to have a significant equity stake. The other prod to better performance was the huge debt the company shouldered. Like imminent death, burdensome debt tends to concentrate the mind. The whole capital structure was designed to force production and managerial efficiencies in order to generate the cash flow needed to pay down debt. And, because the equity base was slender, it grew rapidly in value as the debt declined. For many LBOs, the ultimate goal, often achieved, was to take the company public again and make a killing. Many successful LBOs, however, have remained private companies. Other LBOs, of course, have been failures.

In 1983, Henry Kravis told one of this book's authors that he foresaw a time when LBOs would envelop most of corporate America.

That has not occurred, though only six years later, KKR and its limited partners owned 35 companies with total assets of $59 billion. ("At the time," *The Economist* pointed out 10 years later, "only GM, Ford, Exxon and IBM were bigger.") KKR's largest triumph occurred in 1989, when it executed a hostile takeover of RJR Nabisco for $31 billion. This coup resulted in cascades of publicity plus a highly critical best-selling book, followed by a TV movie. But in the end, it was not one of KKR's success stories.

Academic experts were far more favorably disposed toward the LBO phenomenon than were financial journalists. In testimony before a Congressional committee in 1989, Professor Michael Jensen called LBO outfits like KKR and Forstmann Little "a new model of general management" which produced high premiums not only for the old shareholders who were bought out but also for the new shareholders after the company went public again. The premiums attested to the hidden value that had long gone untapped in pre-LBO days. In a celebrated *Harvard Business Review* article that same year, Jensen predicted the "eclipse" of the old-model public corporations.

Jensen's enthusiasm, like Kravis', proved to be excessive. Only a small fraction of America's corporations are under the wing of LBO holding companies. But the LBO contribution has been immense in proving what could be achieved by making managers owners and by burdening them with a debt load that confronted them with the choice of efficiency or bankruptcy. And note: the emphasis was always on cash flow, not EPS.

But while LBOs can be effective taskmasters, they are a cumbersome and expensive way of creating wealth for shareholders. Cumbersome because of the great effort that goes into putting the deals together, and expensive because of the high fees necessary to motivate the LBO firms. Moreover, huge debt discourages risk taking until the debt comes down. A simpler and far more flexible instrument is the one we advance in this book—Economic Value Added, to which we now turn.

Chapter 2

The Solution

What is Economic Value Added? The short definition, useful at cocktail parties when friends inquire about the book one is writing, is that EVA is the profit that remains after deducting the cost of the capital invested to generate that profit. As Roberto Goizueta, the late CEO of Coca-Cola, an early convert to EVA, once put it, "You only get richer if you invest money at a higher return than the cost of that money to you." And the cost of capital in the EVA equation includes equity capital as well as debt capital. Calculating the cost of debt is easy—it is basically the interest rate paid on a firm's new debt. The equity calculation is more complex, as we shall see, and it varies with the risk the shareholder incurs.

As a concept, however, EVA is simple and easy enough for non-financial types to grasp and to apply, which is one of its virtues. Nor is EVA a new concept: it is what economists have long called economic profit. But what had been lacking until recent years was a method to measure EVA and, equally important, a finely calibrated incentive compensation system, based on EVA improvement, to motivate managers and other employees. After a lengthy period of gestation, EVA was launched by Stern Stewart & Co. in 1989.

Since then, more than 300 companies worldwide adopted the discipline—among them are Coca-Cola, Quaker Oats, Boise Cascade, Briggs & Stratton, Lafarge, Siemens, Tate & Lyle, Telecom New Zealand, Telstra, Monsanto, SPX, Herman Miller, JCPenney, and the U.S. Postal Service.

Properly implemented in a company, EVA aligns the interests of managers with those of shareholders, thereby ending the inherent conflict of interest that has long plagued corporations and that Berle and Means highlighted nearly 70 years ago. The coincidence of interest occurs, in the first instance, because the measurement of corporate performance is no longer affected by the caprice of accounting conventions, not to say gimmickry. Real economic profit is now the measure of corporate performance—clearly, a goal that benefits stockholders. And managers now have the same goal, for their bonuses are tied to EVA. They no longer have an interest in manipulating EPS or RONA or ROI.

EVA is the prime mover of shareholder value, but there is another measure, also originated by Stern Stewart, that precisely captures the gains or losses accruing to a company's shareholders. It is called Market Value Added (MVA) and is defined as the difference between the market value of a company and the sums invested in it over the years. To determine market value, equity is taken at the market price on the date the calculation is made, and debt at book value. The total investment in the company since day one is then calculated—interest-bearing debt and equity, including retained earnings. Present market value is then compared with total investment. In other words, the moneys the investors put in are compared with the funds they can take out. If the latter amount is greater than the former, the company has created wealth. If not, it has destroyed wealth. Cash in, cash out—another simple concept that recalls the grocer's cigar box described in the first chapter. Recently, MVA has also been called Management Value Added, because it is the value added to the net assets for which management is held accountable.

There is a significant link between EVA growth and growth in MVA. Rising EVA tends to foreshadow increases in MVA, though there is no one-to-one correlation mainly because stock market prices reflect not current performance but investors' expectations about the future. Put another way, the basic theory is that MVA is the present value of future expected EVA. If expectations turn out to be unrealistic, then it could be argued that the present-day price was too high or too low. But the key point is that there is a very strong correlation between changes in MVA and changes in EVA. In fact, the correlation is three times better than the correlation between changes in MVA and earnings per share or cash flow, and twice as good as the correlation with return on equity.

At Stern Stewart, the EVA system had its roots in a long-standing preoccupation with the economic model of the firm rather than the accounting model. That is, in the company's consulting work—it advised on valuations of capital projects and acquisitions, capital structure, and dividend policy—the emphasis was always on cash flows, specifically the net present value (NPV) of future free cash flows, a term first coined by Joel Stern in 1972. The theoretical basis for this approach was provided by academic papers published between 1958 and 1961 by two financial economists, Merton H. Miller and Franco Modigliani, both of whom won Nobel prizes in economics. They argued that economic income was the source of value creation in the firm and that the threshold rate of return (we've called it the cost of capital) is determined by the amount of risk the investor assumes—a subject we will later explore in some detail. They also demonstrated, among other things, that investors react rationally to these realities. This is another way of saying that what we like to call the "lead steers"—sophisticated investors with highly developed analytic skills or superior access to new information—lead the investment herd in market movements that respond to changes in the fundamentals.

But one thing that Miller and Modigliani did not do was provide a technique to measure economic income in a firm. At Stern

Stewart, the solution did not immediately suggest itself either. Cash flow analysis was essential in its valuation work, but was not helpful in measuring year-to-year changes in a company's economic income. In analyzing a proposed capital project, for example, you discount to present value its future free cash flows, using an appropriate interest rate (a similar process, in reverse, to what you do when you take a sum of money and calculate how it will grow, through compounded interest, in 10 or 20 years). Then you compare that net present value with the cost of the project and determine whether it is a wise investment.

You can put a value on an entire business in the same fashion. But discounting future free cash flows to NPV is a static measure—it compresses the foreseeable future to today's value rather than providing a year-to-year measure. It would be possible, of course, to compare the NPV of a company in year one with its NPV in year two and see whether there has been a gain or loss. But the problem with this approach is that you are discounting assumed future cash flows, and such assumptions about the future can obviously be wrong.

A number of people at Stern Stewart saw the benefit of a single period-by-period contemporaneous measure of performance. In particular, G. Bennett Stewart III, the senior partner in the firm, made a significant conceptual breakthrough in formulating the concept of EVA (although it followed the developments that had already appeared in Section 3 of Modigliani and Miller's seminal paper on valuation and dividend policy, especially their now-famous footnote 15).* Stripping away their complicated mathematics, EVA stares at us from the pages of their paper. The virtue of EVA is that it is a system for gauging corporate performance based on hard data rather

---

* Stewart's contribution also had its underpinnings in papers presented in J. Stern's *Analytical Methods in Financial Planning* (1972), where the annual calculation of EVA was first suggested.

than projections. EVA is defined as net operating profit after tax (NOPAT) less a capital charge that reflects a firm's cost of capital. Thus, if a company's capital is $5,000 and its cost is 12 percent, the capital charge is $600. If NOPAT, let us say, is $1,000, the $600 charge is deducted and the result is an EVA of $400.

To do the entire exercise, one must first determine the company's cost of capital, often called the required rate of return. That is the rate that compensates investors for their perceived risk, and it naturally varies from industry to industry, from company to company, and even from project to project within a firm. If the company's profits are only equal to the required rate of return, the investor has not made any money—he has not earned economic profit. He only makes an economic profit if the company earns more than the cost of its capital.

Calculating that cost can be a complex exercise, but its essence is simple. The cost of debt capital is the interest on the company's borrowings. Inasmuch as interest is tax-deductible, the after-tax rate is used. On the equity side, the calculation starts with the interest on a long-term government bond—say, 6 percent. That's what the investor can earn on the safest investment imaginable. To that is added the equity risk premium, which varies greatly by industry—generally, from one to seven percentage points. (Obviously, the risk of investing in a grocery chain is much less than investing in a movie production company. Determining the precise appropriate risk premium can be a complicated matter and is best left to the experts.) After the cost of equity has been calculated, the company's "blended" cost of capital is derived from the proportions of debt and equity in its capital structure. In most cases, based on interest rates prevailing in mid-2000, the blended cost comes to between 10 percent and 13 percent.

Some companies rather naively believe that if they substantially raise the proportion of debt to equity, they will reduce the average cost of their capital to something like the same degree, because of the tax subsidy of debt. Not so. They can gain some advantage, but it is not large, for two reasons:

1. The lenders have to pay tax, and their interest rate reflects that—unless the demand for loans is weak and they have to shave their profit margins.
2. The assumption of more debt raises the shareholders' risk, which, in turn, increases the cost of the equity capital. The fact that there may be some advantage in taking on more debt is due to the fact that there are a significant number of lenders that do not pay tax, such as pension funds and non-profit organizations.

After the cost of capital is determined, the next step is to calculate the capital charge that is to be deducted from NOPAT. It is simply the firm's total capital multiplied by its cost, as our example showed.

Now let us look more closely at NOPAT, a key ingredient in the equation. At first glance, the term may sound redundant, for *net* normally means after tax. Here, net refers to adjustments to eliminate various accounting distortions. If we simply used the accountants' bottom line, NOPAT would understate true economic profit, for accounting rules treat as current expenses too many items that, from a shareholder's standpoint, should properly be on the balance sheet as assets. The staff at Stern Stewart have found over 120 accounting "anomalies," as they are politely called, but most companies require no more than a dozen adjustments to make their NOPATs realistic. The rule for making an adjustment is that it is material, will have an effect on management behavior, is easy to understand, and will have a significant impact on the firm's market value.

Among the most common adjustments are three that have been mentioned in the first chapter: (1) research and development

(R&D) costs, (2) advertising and promotion, and (3) staff training and development. Accountants expense R&D, presumably because these outlays would be worth nothing if the firm went belly-up. That consideration is undoubtedly of interest to lenders concerned with liquidation value, but it is totally unrealistic in calculating the true profitability of a company. R&D is properly considered an investment that will bring future returns. Under EVA, it is included in the company's balance sheet and is amortized over the period of years during which these research outlays are expected to have an impact. Only the yearly amortization charge is included as a cost item in deriving NOPAT.

The EVA treatment is the same for advertising and promotion expenses for consumer goods companies such as Coca-Cola and Johnson & Johnson. To be sure, advertising and promotion have a shorter life span than R&D, but these outlays are also an investment that builds long-term proprietary value in the form of new products and trademarks.

Taxes show up in the NOPAT calculation only in the year in which they are paid—in contrast to accounting custom, which deducts them in the year in which they were deferred. Such taxes are, of course, a debt that the company has to pay in the future. Thus, accountants' deduction of these future obligations may well be commendably conservative, but the practice distorts the company's operating results for any one year. Limiting the tax deduction to the amount actually paid gives a far more realistic view of the year's costs. The same considerations apply to the reserves that accountants set up, such as a reserve to pay the costs of fulfilling warranty obligations. If the reserve is too large, it will artificially depress earnings; if it is too modest, it will inflate earnings. One can get an accurate picture only by listing the actual disbursement for warranties during the year.

Accelerated depreciation is another *bête noir* in EVA accounting. A company's tax department likes accelerated depreciation because it reduces taxes by jamming more costs into fewer years. But, by the same token, it reduces earnings. For many companies, straight-line depreciation is adequate, for it mirrors actual obsolescence reasonably well. But straight-line depreciation creates distortions for companies with a lot of heavy, long-lasting equipment, inasmuch as it makes the durable old equipment seem cheaper than new equipment that may be more efficient. To solve this problem, EVA uses sinking fund depreciation. The annual charge does not vary from year to year, but, as in the case of a mortgage, the return of principal is small in the early years but dominates the later years, reflecting the actual decline in the economic value of plant and equipment toward the end. This adjustment is mirrored, of course, by steeply declining asset values on the balance sheet in later years. For capital-intensive companies, the adjustment can be enormous.

Other accounting changes affect the balance sheet alone. Under EVA, the full price paid for acquisitions is recorded on the balance sheet, even if the pooling of interest method (described in Chapter 1) is used. Under the pooling method, the "goodwill" premium does not show up, which may encourage overpayment. Only if the full price paid is placed on the asset side can we expect managers to impose practical limits on the prices they pay for acquisitions, especially if their incentives are tied to EVA.

EVA provides stern restraints on the profligate use of capital. That was its main attraction for Tate & Lyle, a global giant in sweeteners and starches, which is headquartered in London. "In the past," says Simon Gifford, the company's finance director, "we had emphasized profitability, especially earnings per share, because of the demands of the City and the analysts." Financial types like Gifford did focus on cash, but operations managers primarily looked at earnings. The consequence, says Gifford, was that "as a company we were not paying enough attention to our capital base, particularly our working capital." EVA was obviously a way to set priorities right—and it did. Apart from tightening up on the use of working capital, Tate & Lyle shed several operations that showed up with negative EVA, which meant that they weren't returning their cost of capital and had no reasonable prospects of doing so in the future. "If it had not been for EVA," says Gifford, "some of these disposal decisions would not have been taken until later years."

One of the virtues of EVA is its adaptability. Not only is it a measurement system for a company as a whole, but it can readily be broken down to the level of a division, a factory, a store, or even a product line. It can be used wherever an allocation of revenues, costs, and capital employed—the hardest part—can be made. Centura Banks, Inc., a bank holding company in Rocky Mount, North Carolina, has worked out EVA not only for every product line and every branch, but also for all of its customers, which enables it to concentrate on the most profitable ones. The J.D. Group, a chain of over 500 retail furniture stores in South Africa, makes a monthly EVA calculation for every store manager. Almost all EVA companies take the calculation down to at least the divisional level.

As a measurement system, EVA is not only a guide and a prod to managers seeking to maximize returns, but also a godsend to investors trying to determine the reality behind the maze of accounting numbers that the SEC compels companies to publish. Most EVA companies also publish their EVA numbers, generally with a trend line dating back a few years. Some companies have gone even further, publishing their full EVA calculations in their annual reports. Equifax, the Atlanta-based financial data reporting company, was the first to do so, followed by Herman Miller, Inc., the celebrated Michigan furniture manufacturer. In its 1998 annual report, Miller's lengthy EVA presentation preceded the pages devoted to the accounting tables. A growing number of financial houses are now using the EVA framework in their company reports, to supplement more traditional analysis. Among them are Goldman Sachs, Credit Suisse First Boston, Salomon Smith Barney, Morgan Stanley, Banque Paribas, Oppenheimer Capital, J.B. Were & Son, and the Macquarie Bank.

Goldman Sachs has gone so far as to work out the EVA calculation for the whole of the Standard & Poor's 500 index—one of the factors that led it to believe that share prices were not too high during the past few years.

EVA, however, is far more than a measurement tool. It is also the basis of an incentive compensation system that puts managers on the same footing as shareholders, rewarding them for actions that increase shareholder returns and penalizing them for failure. The core of the plan is the establishment of goals and timetables for EVA improvement. Goals are typically set in advance for a three- or five-year period, to avoid the annual bargaining that characterizes many corporate bonus plans. That bargaining process between supervisor and subordinate has the fatal weakness that the target agreed to is one that is likely to be met without great effort, producing a bonus for little more than average achievement. We call this scoring an easy "B" when an "A" or "A+" is possible.

In the EVA system, the goal is generally called the "expected improvement" for the year. If it is achieved, the managers receive 100 percent of a "target bonus." If they fall short of the goal but make 60 percent or 70 percent of it, the bonus is reduced proportionately. But if the shortfall is too great (the figure varies from plan to plan), they receive nothing. On the other hand, if they do better than the expected EVA improvement for the year, they are entitled to an "excess bonus" roughly proportional to the superior achievement. Some end up with a multiple two or three times the target bonus. At SPX, a Michigan-based diversified manufacturer, several awards have exceeded seven times base salary.

This can amount to a good deal of money. The target bonus is a sum equivalent to a percentage of salary; it generally ranges from 100 percent for the CEO to 10 percent for the lowest ranks. Most managers get around 50 percent. Top executives are judged by the performance of the entire company; managers are compensated according to the showing of their division or unit. The only exception is usually the chief divisional executive, who receives 25 percent of his or her bonus based on corporate results, and 75 percent based on divisional results. The split is meant to encourage cooperation with other divisions. It is a generous system, which reverses the imbalance of most executive compensation systems, in which a person's fixed pay is far greater than the variable. By changing the proportions, the EVA system puts executives at considerable personal risk and prods them to strenuous efforts.

Moreover, in the ideal EVA plan, the bonus is "uncapped." Many corporate compensation committees balk at this generosity, fearing stockholder complaints and a bad press, yet it is easily justified. While executives are enriched, it is only by a process that also enriches shareholders. At Armstrong World Industries, the floor coverings empire headquartered in Lancaster, Pennsylvania, it was hard to begrudge executives who received more than twice their target bonuses in 1995—the year their share price rose 60 percent. Herman Miller's executives did even better, quintupling their target bonuses in the fiscal years 1997 and 1998. Meantime, Miller's share price tripled.

Another significant feature of the EVA incentive system is the bonus "bank"—the repository of a good chunk, or all, of the annual bonus, to be doled out in later years, depending on the level of performance. In one popular version of the bank, one-third of the "excess" bonus is banked and two-thirds distributed in cash. If the next year sees a drop in EVA, the bank is debited with one third of any remaining funds paid out.

In another version, the so-called "all-in" bank, the entire bonus is sequestered, to be drawn down one-third each year. (The bank is prefunded so that there can be a first-year payout.) Both versions of the bank have the virtue of putting much of the executives' compensation at risk for an extended period, and making the award dependent on future performance. The "all-in" bank has the distinct advantage of putting more money—the entire bonus—at risk. Both schemes are designed to ensure that managers take the long view. There is no point in seeking quick short-term results—for example, by shrinking the capital base, for the down years that follow would wipe out the one-time gain.

For the top tier of executives, there is an additional incentive plan: leveraged stock options (LSOs). Under this plan, a chunk of the annual bonus is distributed in the form of stock options. The executive gets more options than would normally be available at the price, which is one reason it is called leveraged. But, unlike normal options, which have a fixed strike price, LSOs can only be exercised at ever higher prices year by year. Otherwise they are worthless. This ensures that executives cannot be enriched by options unless stockholders are also enriched in roughly the same degree by rising share prices.

In sum, all these plans are designed to put executives at the same risk as stockholders. Actually, the risk can be even greater for the managers. Shareholders are dependent on the returns for the entire company, as are the top executives. But divisional managers, as has been mentioned, receive bonuses based on their parochial performance. They can lose out if their own unit falters, even as the rest of the company prospers. That happened, for example, at one unit of SPX in 1997. The following year, the division was turned around.

The EVA bonus system usually starts with the top managers and is gradually extended through the ranks of middle management. In some pioneering companies—Herman Miller, Briggs & Stratton, and SPX—the plan has been taken right down to the shop floor. How this form of employee capitalism is engineered is a subject for later exploration.

Chapter 3

The Need for a Winning Strategy and Organization

The adoption of a fully articulated EVA program—a measurement program, a management system, plus an incentive compensation plan, together with a thoroughgoing training operation—is often critical to a corporation's success. But it is not a sufficient condition for that success. Not surprisingly, a company must also have a winning strategy and an appropriate organization. A sophisticated EVA system will be of no great utility if, for example, a company lacks a clear marketing thrust, if it has an imprecise sense of the customer base it is seeking, if its products lack a niche or some competitive advantage, either in cost or perceived superiority, or if, in the case of a commodity producer, it cannot demonstrate that it does a better job than its rivals in serving customers. Nor will a firm meet the EVA challenge with a dysfunctional organization.

A new company can hardly prosper without an adequate strategic plan to best the competition, at least to the point of attaining a sufficient market share. And an established company often falters when it persists with a once splendid strategy that is no longer relevant in a changed environment.

Briggs & Stratton Corporation provides a useful case study of the interplay between strategic innovation and the EVA discipline in restoring prosperity to an old-line company that had lost its way. With $1.3 billion in sales, B&S is the world's largest producer of air-cooled, gasoline engines. The company, founded in Milwaukee in 1908, had a colorful past and decades of prosperity after World War II—until 1989, when it plunged into the red for the first time since the 1920s. That led to dramatic changes.

First, some background. Innovation always characterized Briggs & Stratton. Its founders were Stephen F. Briggs, who was 23 in 1908, and Harold M. Stratton, who was 29. Briggs, an electrical engineer, was one of those inspired tinkerers who keep the U.S. Patent Office prosperous; Stratton was already a seasoned businessman with interests in the grain trade. What brought them together was a design by Briggs of a six-cylinder, two-cycle auto engine that they apparently thought would sweep the industry. It soon became clear, however, that it would be too costly to produce. But Briggs & Stratton were not about to be denied their flyer into the auto business. This was an era, after all, when ambitious machine shops were turning out cars all over the country. So the two partners decided to build a four-cylinder car from parts purchased from various vendors—engine, frame, body, everything. Never modest, they called their product the Superior, but the project failed and they produced only two touring cars and one roadster.

Still determined to participate in the burgeoning auto business, they then became parts suppliers. Briggs designed an electrical engine-igniter, which went on the market in 1909 and sold well. Other electrical parts followed; an all-purpose switch became a best seller. They also bought the rights to the "motor wheel," developed it further, and advertised it widely. A small gasoline engine attached to a wheel, its widest use was as a third wheel to power bicycles, but it also propelled sleds and became the power source for the Flyer, a minicar that consisted of a wooden-slat floor, four wheels, two seats, a steering column, and the motor wheel in back; it had no roof or doors. Some 2,000 were sold before the contraption was discontinued in 1924.

The motor wheel, while a financial failure, did lead to the development of a small, stationary gasoline engine, which went through various model changes and won acceptance as a power source for garden tractors, lawn mowers, pumps, and other small farm equipment, as well as washing machines, for which there was a great demand in rural areas that lacked electricity. Another winner, starting in the 1920s, was a line of automobile locks which the company manufactured for years until the operation was spun off in 1995.

After World War II, the massive population shift to suburbia powered Briggs & Stratton's success. As millions discovered the joys of greensward and garden, there was a great demand for lawn mowers, especially those driven by engines. B&S's aluminum die-cast engine, lighter and cheaper than its predecessors, was introduced in 1953 and became wildly popular. The company's expansion was rapid. By the mid-1980s, B&S had a two million-square-foot factory in Wauwatosa, a suburb of Milwaukee, and was employing 10,000. The workforce was unionized, labor costs were high, productivity was hamstrung by onerous work rules, and the company suffered a series of costly strikes.

To reduce labor costs, B&S spent a fortune on automated equipment during the 1980s. Automation was one of the greatest "cash traps" of the era. Whatever the "issue du jour" was for CEOs, the automation peddlers were there to offer the solution: "We will automate you to competitiveness"—"We will automate you out of your labor problems"—or "We will automate your quality problems out of the process." If you just had faith, automation would change your economic life forever. But was it costly! The experience of Briggs & Stratton was representative of that of many other capital-intensive manufacturers in the 1980s. In the late 1970s, the ratio of capital invested in operating assets to net income at B&S was about 3-to-1. By the late 1980s, that ratio had ballooned to over 9-to-1.

Much of the money went for automation of what can only be called "bad process." As has become clear with hindsight, many of the high value-creating firms of today are the ones that survived the automation cash trap. They learned that they had to fix the process first. Then, but only then, could they automate those aspects of the process that showed the best promise.

As automation was consuming capital, the competitive situation was becoming more difficult. While B&S was losing its position as the cost leader in the industry, it also faced increasing pressure from Japan, where labor was much cheaper, as well as from its primary domestic competitor, which, by the late 1980s, had achieved an estimated 30 percent labor cost advantage over B&S. Even more significant was a shift in the pattern of retail sales, from independent dealers to mass market merchandisers like Wal-Mart, Kmart, and Home Depot. These outfits were much more insistent than the old-line dealers on exacting the lowest possible price and had the bargaining power to work their will. In fiscal 1989 (ending June 30), Briggs & Stratton showed a loss of over $20 million.

It was a shock, but the company had seen it coming for at least 12 months. A thorough overhaul of strategy and organization was ordered by chief executive Frederick Stratton (grandson of the co-founder) in 1988. Around the same time, Stern Stewart & Co. was brought in to make valuations of various components of the company, with a view to asset sales or spin-offs. The company also feared a hostile takeover and had Stern Stewart look into the feasibility of a leveraged buyout by the company's executives.

That idea was discarded, and the company concentrated on reordering its priorities and conserving capital. It also adopted a full EVA program. Outlining the new approach, a memo developed in the course of the strategic planning process stated: "I do not believe we can be all things to all people. We must pick our punches." Briggs & Stratton had long been the cost leader in the industry for high-volume basic small engines, but in recent years it had ventured into the high end of the market, only to lose money consistently. "I think we've proven that we cannot profitably serve as an engine 'job shop' for the upscale OEMs [original equipment manufacturers]," the memo argued. "The low-volume, high-featured segments of the industry are characterized by the presence of numerous aggressive players (primarily Japanese), with superior design engineering skills, and low barriers to entry."

On the other hand, the high-volume, low-cost end of the industry, which offered engines without unnecessary bells and whistles, was populated by two companies: B&S and a considerably smaller competitor, Tecumseh. And barriers to entry were high, because of the capital requirements. "It seems axiomatic," the memo concluded, "that the likelihood of high returns is greater on those battlefields where there is only one currently viable competitor, and where a high learning curve and economies of scale serve as a significant . . . barrier to potential entrants. If we scrupulously adhere to this scope, I think it is highly unlikely we would ever see an offshore frontal assault. . . . If we deviate from that scope, such a move by both offshore and domestic competitors becomes much more likely, as [our] resources are stretched and the competitive edge is lost."

The decision was taken to concentrate all efforts on the value end of the market. That was to be B&S's core business, and it would strive to again become the industry's broad-scope cost leader. If there were to be any forays beyond the core business, the company decided that it would only be in a joint venture requiring a relatively modest investment and with a partner that already had a competitive edge in the relevant niche.

To become the cost leader and to boost sales with the Wal-Marts and Kmarts, Briggs & Stratton needed to economize on both the use of capital and labor costs. The EVA discipline focused attention on the total cost of capital for the first time in the corporation's history. But it was not enough for that constraint to be felt in the executive suite; the discipline had to be thrust down into the operating units.

That was the logic of the thoroughgoing reorganization of the company that ensued. In the old days, when the mission was producing more or less generic engines with near-universal market acceptance, a functional, vertically integrated organization was undoubtedly the most efficient. Little corporate planning was required beyond planning for operational capacity. By the 1980s, however, the small-engine industry began to show a much higher level of uncertainty and complexity—and the size and complexity of the company's internal operations increased as well. Changing the company's organizational design in response to this increase in complexity was critical to its future.

Under Stratton, the company that had long been the epitome of vertical integration was restructured into seven separate operating divisions, such as the small-engine division (small engines powering walk-behind lawn mowers), the large-engine division (engines for ride-on lawn mowers and commercial applications), a division that makes aluminum castings and another that produces iron castings, and so on. The divisions were given a large grant of autonomy, not only for operational matters but also for capital expenditures. By pushing decision making down to this level, the company accomplished a dramatic improvement in cash flow and capital management. Managers became acutely aware of the cost of capital and how it affected their performance—which was now the divisional EVA result. Their annual bonuses were now, in part, dependent on that figure, which tended to concentrate attention. The basic formula for all divisional executives calls for 50 percent of bonus to be based on corporate results, 40 percent on divisional EVA, and 10 percent on appraisal of personal performance by a superior. Bonuses for corporate staff are based 100 percent on corporate performance, but again with the option to base 10 percent on personal performance criteria. The incentive plan for executive staff also has a bonus bank, and top managers, in addition, have leveraged stock options.

Financial improvement, in turn, reflected a number of important changes that flowed from restructuring: better focus on the product line; more thorough integration of cross-functional initiatives; better assessment of labor/capital trade-offs; and, not to be minimized, the development of more seasoned and resourceful managers as a result of enhanced responsibility. EVA analysis played a key role in all corporate decisions—divestitures, the establishment of new factories in the hinterland, and strategic alliances in China, India, and Japan.

Over the years, decentralization was accompanied by shop-floor initiatives that had not been encouraged before. After a good deal of labor turmoil (covered in a later chapter), the hourly-rated workers in Wauwatosa have a modified form of EVA written into their union contracts. Rank-and-file representatives participate in process-improvement teams, which quantify their proposed savings in the standard EVA format. The Spectrum division in Wauwatosa, which makes specialized parts for other divisions, has a high level of worker participation and seems in a continual buzz with process-improvement teams.

The new strategic emphasis, decentralization, and the EVA discipline led to continual improvements. In 1989, just before adoption of its EVA program, Briggs & Stratton's negative EVA was a whopping $62 million. In fiscal 1993, the company achieved a positive EVA for the first time in many years. It earned a 12.9 percent return on capital, with a calculated cost of capital of 12 percent. The company never turned back. It has earned the cost of capital in each fiscal year since 1993, including a record $50.9 million EVA in FY 1999. Shareholders have had a most agreeable ride. Anyone who bought $100 worth of stock in the fall of 1990 at $10.25 per share would have had $673 in hand in May 1999.

The Briggs & Stratton story underscores the importance of corporate strategy. The company's revival would hardly have been likely if the company had merely adopted EVA but persisted with a muddled strategy and an archaic structure. What generalizations can be drawn from the B&S experience?

The basic principle involved in developing a successful corporate strategy is to identify an appropriate competitive position—in other words, to define the firm's "core business"—and then to dedicate virtually all of the organization's time, resources, people, and capital to building and maintaining that position. Devoting substantial human and physical capital resources to noncore segments will generally dilute a company's competitive advantage, unless the activity is conducted in an alliance with a partner that has a special competence in that segment. Briggs & Stratton, for example, has a joint venture with the Daihatsu Motor Company in Japan and a long-term contract with Mitsubishi to produce high-priced, premium engines, which B&S formerly manufactured at a loss in the United States.

Well-researched and practical insights into corporate strategy are of relatively recent vintage. The seminal work in the area, and still very much the strategic bible, is Michael Porter's *Competitive Strategy*, published in 1980. Porter introduces the concept of industry analysis, which requires a determination of the intensity of five forces that drive competition in an industry: (1) the threat of new entrants; (2) buyer power; (3) supplier power; (4) the threat of substitute products; and (5) the level of rivalry among existing firms. After an analysis of these five forces, which determines the attractiveness of the industry, Porter develops the concepts of competitive positioning and scope as the principal means of outperforming other firms.

Porter identifies two major competitive positions. The first is "cost leadership," which requires "aggressive construction of efficient-scale facilities, vigorous pursuit of cost reductions . . . tight cost and overhead control, avoidance of marginal customer accounts, cost minimization in areas like R&D, service, sales force, advertising, and so on." The second competitive position he labels "differentiation," which means "creating something that is perceived *industrywide* as being unique," such as distinctive designs, brand image, technology, quality, or customer service.

Porter's work has shown that companies that are incapable of achieving either of these competitive positions are unlikely to be successful. Such firms, in his words, "lack the market share, capital investment and resolve to play the low-cost game [or] the industrywide differentiation necessary to obviate the need for a low-cost position . . . the firm stuck in the middle is almost guaranteed low profitability . . . [and] . . . probably suffers from a blurred corporate culture and a conflicting set of organizational arrangements and motivational system."

In addition to a firm's competitive position, Porter stresses the importance of market share, which elsewhere he has called scope. He observes that, in many industries, there is a U-shaped relationship between return on investment and scope. Companies with either exceptionally broad or narrow scope tend to produce high ROIs, while medium-scope firms experience low returns. This suggests that firms can be "stuck in the middle" in terms of market share as well as competitive positioning.

In later work, Porter recognized four basic strategies that are most likely to result in superior value creation over the long run: (1) broad-scope cost leadership (Wal-Mart in the 1990s is a good example); (2) broad-scope differentiation (IBM in the 1970s); (3) narrow-scope cost leadership (Volkswagen in the 1960s); and (4) narrow-scope differentiation (Cray Computers in the 1980s). Briggs & Stratton opted for broad-scope cost leadership and has been able to maintain it.

But as the experiences of Wal-Mart, IBM, Volkswagen, and Cray suggest, it is an enormous challenge to sustain a high-value competitive position and scope. Over time, the industry may "shift away" from your choice of positioning, in which case your organization is likely to lose focus and fail to sustain its position. Coach Vince Lombardi, of National Football League fame, once said that it is more difficult to maintain than it is to achieve; the second or third NFL championship is an accomplishment made all the more difficult by both the natural tendency toward complacency and the continuous shift in the game strategies of competing teams. A periodic soul-searching is in order for firms that are committed to delivering value over the long term.

The Porter analysis has been criticized by some as too simplistic, and, in fact, Porter has refined his own model to reflect the research conducted in the intervening years. But his approach nevertheless represents a good starting point for the discussion of strategic focus. Some noted strategists have enhanced the Porter analysis with the concept of the "resource-based view of the firm," which holds that a necessary condition to sustaining a competitive advantage is to maintain resources that are valuable, scarce, hard to imitate, and relatively immobile. Perhaps the most important element of strategy is for the firm to properly identify these key resources (i.e., core competencies) and to exploit them in a way that maximizes value creation.

Probably the best recent book on the development of high-value strategies—a work that contains a model, analysis, and vernacular uniquely suited to companies attempting to manage for value creation—is Michael Treacy's and Fred Wiersema's *The Discipline of Market Leaders*, published in 1995. In building on Porter's insight that a firm cannot deliver superior returns by trying to be all things to all people, Treacy and Wiersema identify three "value disciplines" and their operating models:

1. Cost leadership (and the associated model of "operational excellence");

2. Product leadership (with its operating model of "innovation and commercialization"); and

3. Best total solution (and its operating model of "customer intimacy").

The description of these generic strategies as "value disciplines" is a linguistic bull's-eye. It recognizes that the necessity of choosing one of these three strategies goes to the heart of the firm's primary mission: creating value. And it draws attention to the rigorous discipline that is required to sustain the high-value position.

Treacy and Wiersema's definitions of the value disciplines correspond closely to those developed by Michael Porter, except that they divide the differentiation strategy into two distinct disciplines: (1) product leadership and (2) best total solution. This distinction turns on the concept of the "expanded product," which encompasses not only the features of the product itself, but how it is marketed, delivered, serviced, and supported. The product leader delivers a product or service so unique in value in and of itself that a premium may be exacted for it in the marketplace. The best total-solution player will be so adept at developing the right mix of price, features, product support, and the like, for individual customers or a group of customers, that it will similarly realize a superior value in its markets.

The choice of value discipline is the most fundamental decision management must make. Arriving at the best decision requires careful analysis of the company's strengths, culture, organizational structure, motivation systems, and marketing channels, and of how its capabilities compare with current opportunities. A good alignment of internal capabilities with external market opportunities is critical for success. In other words, the opportunities must be real, and the company must have the competencies necessary to exploit them—or at least there must be a plan to build those capabilities that has a reasonable chance of success.

It is easy to take the wrong direction. A while back, a management consultant from an accounting firm was conducting a road show that he called "linking corporate strategy to EVA." His main focus was on identifying a company's core competencies and developing a "strategic architecture" that attempted to make the most of those competencies by applying them in other markets—in other words, "strategic diversification." The problem with this approach, however, is that a company's core competencies constitute only one factor that should determine the choice of value discipline. In practice, strategic decision making based solely on this factor is a prescription for overinvestment and destruction of shareholder value.

Ironically, the consultant persisted for a long time in citing with approval the diversification strategy of at least one company that has clearly failed to earn its cost of capital and to produce adequate shareholder returns over several business cycles. Ignoring the imperative to add value is a dangerous proposition for management. Effective strategic decision making must ensure that there is a payoff for shareholders at the end of the day.

Another significant contribution by Treacy and Wiersema is the concept that, regardless of which of the three value disciplines the firm adopts as its strategic focus, it must maintain at least minimal standards in executing the other disciplines. In other words, product leaders cannot simply ignore costs, and companies dedicated to providing the best total solution must still have acceptable products. All this may seem elementary when spelled out, but it is amazing how many companies overlook the obvious.

What is the minimal, or "threshold," level of performance required in the nonchosen disciplines? That level is achieved when the firm performs "ably and adequately" in those areas, so as not to detract from its achievements in its chosen discipline. Thus, a firm must have a keen sense of its industry and understand its threshold requirements. It must understand the levels of price, product, and service that are necessary. At the same time, it must attempt to meet such requirements without squandering human and capital resources above the threshold level.

A discussion of what it takes to develop a high-value strategy would not be complete without a discussion of the role of growth in formulating strategy. Executives of firms experiencing significant growth in revenues but less than stellar stock performance often voice the criticism that value management is "antigrowth"—that it stifles innovation by forcing capital to be "managed down" for maximum return. Top-line growth is not by itself any evidence of shareholder value added. Revenue growth without capital discipline destroys value, which explains why so many once successful firms "grow" their way into oblivion. But it is also true that companies that merely continue to earn the cost of capital on a stable or deteriorating capital base exhibit MVAs that are less than impressive.

To achieve continuous increases in EVA and MVA, the firm must develop a growth strategy that has reasonable prospects for success. A company that is truly managing for value creation cannot play its cards too close to the chest. The managers need to remind themselves that their shareholders are paying them to take intelligent risks. Once management has embraced a particular value discipline, it has an obligation to explore every avenue of potential growth that is consistent with that discipline and reasonably likely to deliver at least a cost-of-capital return.

There is currently a debate in management circles about whether it pays to "fix" an unprofitable company before pursuing further growth, or whether one should instead keep growing the firm while attempting to fix it. To us, the most defensible position in this debate has come from research by McKinsey's growth practice group. The bottom line of their analysis is that management teams should be forced to "earn the right to grow." In other words, achieving a minimum standard of profitability on existing operations provides the only sound platform for further growth. Another way of interpreting the finding: those companies that have shown a consistent ability to earn more than the cost of capital are most likely to succeed when they expand their range of activities.

To be successful, a firm must not only have an overarching strategy that makes sense; it is equally important to create an organizational structure that furthers the chosen strategy. Form must follow function. A bold new strategy encased in an archaic structure would be hobbled from the start.

One of the most useful guides to the structural design of a business is a two-decade old article entitled "What is the Right Organization Structure?" by Robert Duncan (*Organizational Dynamics*, Winter 1979). Duncan began by observing that organization structure is much more than boxes on a chart that shows reporting responsibilities; rather, it is "a pattern of interactions and coordination that links the technology, tasks, and human components of the organization to ensure that the organization accomplishes its purpose." Duncan identified two basic objectives: (1) expediting internal information exchanges; and (2) coordinating behavior across the various parts of the organization.

For practical purposes, Duncan limited his analysis to the two general types of organizational structure familiar to managers: functional and decentralized. Functional, centralized organizations (i.e., those organized into functional departments such as manufacturing, engineering, purchasing, and the like) tend to be very efficient. They are also supportive of the technical specialties and skill sets required by younger, smaller firms that have a very clear and limited competitive challenge. But Duncan's research indicated that when structure is centralized, information flows are restricted. As a result, the company is less capable of gathering the information it needs when faced with uncertainty. This makes it less likely that the few individuals at the top will have the information required to make the best decisions.

Accordingly, Duncan concluded that, in the case of a firm operating in a relatively simple environment, the functional form of organization is best. Where the firm faces a more complex environment, and that environment can be segmented appropriately to address the complexity, the decentralized organization would be the form of choice. If no effective segmentation is possible, the functional organization becomes the default choice.

In the case of dynamic organizations, some form of lateral, or even cross-functional, relations may be required to help generate needed information or promote integration across segments or functions. Lateral relations range from informal contacts between segment managers or functional managers, to integrators (corporate staff or group executives), to the most complex form: a matrix organization, with its dual authority and dotted-line relationships. Duncan cautioned that the least invasive form of lateral relations that does the trick is the right one. Matrix organizations can become very difficult to manage, in part because they have the unfortunate side effect of obscuring accountability.

For most organizations of any significant size or maturity, segmentation and decentralization are the answers. Truly indivisible organizations, except small ones, are rare. Segmentation may be along geographic, process, product, industry, or customer lines. How do companies embracing the three different value disciplines that we have discussed handle segmentation?

Cost leaders focus on streamlining processes to minimize cost; thus, they tend to standardize operations as much as possible. If processes are not particularly interdependent, as is the case with many commodities, creating separate business units for the several processes is likely to produce the best results. If processes are integral to the product, as in the production of internal combustion engines, segmentation by product is likely to deliver the highest value.

Product leaders, by contrast, are product innovators. They will generally operate better with a more loosely knit, flexible organization divided along product lines, where each segment has all the resources necessary to support product development and commercialization.

The third group of companies—those that embrace the discipline that we have called "best total solution" and focus on customer results and relationship management—will adopt a segmentation based on geography or on customer or industry groups.

In all three groups of companies, those that create the greatest value tend to place capital decisions at the level in the organization where there is the best information to make that assessment. That goal reinforces the benefits of decentralization.

Decentralized decision rights, as they are commonly called, are not all that is needed, as was persuasively demonstrated by the work of Michael C. Jensen and the late William H. Meckling in their seminal article, "Specific and General Knowledge and Organizational Structure," published in the *Journal of Applied Corporate Finance* in its summer 1995 issue. The authors demonstrated that it is not enough simply to delegate decision rights to managers possessing the requisite knowledge to make the right choices. Like other mortals, managers are to a large degree motivated by their own self-interest, and thus a variety of controls and incentives are necessary to insure that managers consistently act in the interests of the firm.

In sum, the article concluded that organizations must establish "internal rules of the game" that not only distribute decision rights to the appropriate people but also impose control mechanisms consisting of "a performance measurement and evaluation system and a reward and punishment system."

Jensen's and Meckling's ideas were subsequently expounded and elaborated in a textbook, *Managerial Economics and Organizational Architecture* published in 1997 by James Brickley, Clifford Smith, and Jerold Zimmerman (hereinafter, "BS&Z"). For a firm to achieve optimal success, the BS&Z book characterizes the three key elements of organizational architecture in these terms: "(1) the assignment of decision rights within the company; (2) the methods of rewarding individuals; and (3) the structure of systems to evaluate the performance of both individuals and business units." The authors draw an analogy between these components and a three-legged stool. All three legs must be designed so that the stool is in balance. Modifying any of these elements without consideration of the other two will most likely contribute to the deterioration of the firm's value.

The BS&Z model starts with the premise that successful firms assign decision rights in ways that effectively link that authority with the information needed to exercise it. At the same time, the organizational architecture must ensure that there are appropriate systems in place to evaluate performance and provide rewards to motivate the desired behavior of individuals.

As we have observed before, the business environment in which a firm operates shapes its strategy, structure, and assignment of decision rights. And the firm's strategy, in combination with its organizational architecture, motivates value-creating behavior by individuals. Figure 3.1 is a version of the BS&Z model. We have customized it for use by those firms which are committed to the integration of the EVA discipline into their organizations.

Drawing further on the BS&Z book, we now discuss each of the three elements of organizational architecture and the considerable challenge faced by companies that are attempting to integrate EVA into their firms while keeping the three-legged stool in balance.

The firm must first resolve the issue of structural configuration. EVA centers are unique in that they require the broadest grant of decision rights relative to the panoply of sub-unit decision assignments. Let us look at those various sub-units first.

1. Cost centers call for the assignment of decision rights to produce a specified output with the greatest efficiency (i.e., the lowest cost). A critical determinant of cost centers is getting the optimal mix of inputs (labor, materials, and purchased services).

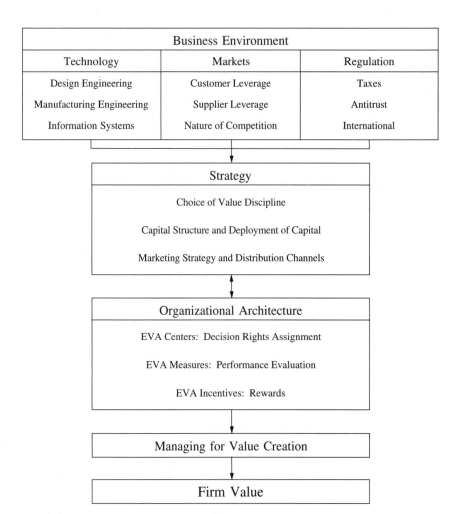

Figure 3.1   The Value-Driving Organizational Architecture

2. Expense centers generally involve sub-units that provide corporate services (accounting, legal, human resources) and are measured on their performance in delivering maximum output relative to cost.

3. Revenue centers are granted decision rights for marketing, selling, and distribution. Performance measurement may be based on various objectives, such as revenue maximization or gross aggregate margins less selling expenses.

4. Profit centers are granted all of the aforementioned decision rights—cost, expense, and revenue—and are given a fixed budget. They are generally established when product mix, output, pricing, and quality decisions require information that is specific to the sub-unit and expensive to transfer. But there is a downside, as BS&Z notes: "Motivating individual profit centers to maximize profits will not generally maximize profits for the firm as a whole when there are interdependencies among business units. For example, individual units focusing on their own profits generally ignore how their actions affect the sales and costs of other units."

5. Investment centers are essentially profit centers that have the additional authority to make capital outlays. Their success is measured by how efficiently they use their capital.

An EVA center can best be described as an investment center where the chosen performance measure is Economic Value Added. To designate a sub-unit as an EVA center, management must believe that value optimization will be achieved if profit and capital expenditure decisions are assigned to the sub-unit, and must be willing to relinquish some control in assigning those decision rights. Failing that, the only EVA center will be the entire firm.

EVA centers should be created only if the sub-unit manager will likely have the optimal product mix, the knowledge needed to select the correct price and quantity, and the most complete information on investment opportunities. Does this mean that the EVA center should then have complete autonomy from corporate management? Certainly not. There are decision rights and there are decision rights.

Drawing on Fama and Jensen's widely cited article, "Separation of Ownership and Control" (*Journal of Law & Economics, 26*, 1983), BS&Z identify four types of decision rights that may be assigned:

"Initiation. Generation of proposals for resource utilization and structuring of contracts.

"Ratification. Choice of the decision initiatives to be implemented.

"Implementation. Execution of ratified decisions.

"Monitoring. Measurement of performance of decision agents and implementation of rewards."

Initiation and implementation rights are characterized by Fama and Jensen as "design management rights." They use "decision control rights" to refer to ratification and monitoring. Granting an agent (i.e., a nonowner employee) both decision management and decision control rights generally leads to suboptimal behavior, to put it mildly. Accordingly, although the assignment of substantial decision management rights to an EVA center is the prerequisite for the establishment of such a center, the retention of decision control rights by senior corporate officers and the board of directors is essential. A rigorous process for ratifying and monitoring the decisions of EVA centers must be developed. Putting EVA centers on auto pilot is a prescription for disaster.

At what level in the organization should the EVA centers be created? The answer will be determined by the size of the firm, where relevant information is located within it, and the extent to which subordinate units are self-contained and ably led. The unparalleled growth in the reliability and quality of information systems in the past several years has made decentralized management much more feasible than in the past. The adoption of the EVA language and culture can also reduce the cost of transferring information within the firm.

In the wake of its decision to adopt EVA, the management of Briggs & Stratton was faced with the task of identifying the proper number and scope of EVA centers. As previously mentioned, it set up seven autonomous divisions. Taking the large-engine division

(LED) as an example, we can better understand the company's rationale in defining these divisions. The LED encompasses the firm's utility and ride-on mower engines in the 5- to 20-horsepower range, producing the majority of such mower and lawn tractor engines in the world today. The company had three main reasons for making LED an EVA center: (1) the horsepower range represents a natural break from the company's other operations; (2) the ride-on mower, lawn tractor, and utility businesses are somewhat less seasonal than the more mass-market walk-behind lawn mower business; and (3) LED had about $550 million in annual sales and 2,600 employees, a level that is practical in terms of the span of control and development of sub-unit information systems.

A few years back, at a meeting of the EVA Institute, a Stern Stewart affiliate, which annually brings together several-score EVA companies, one of the hottest topics of discussion was the type and level of EVA measures (and, by corollary, incentives) that should be implemented in the firm. Can direct EVA measures be implemented effectively on the shop floor? Should the firm consider the use of "value drivers" (elements of the production and sales processes that can contribute to economic value) at some levels? We believe that the answers to these questions should be determined by reference to the BS&Z model. In other words, are we properly matching performance measurement with the assignment of decision rights? The application of direct EVA measures to a cost center would be a mistake because cost centers have no control over capital expenditures, which is a key determinant of EVA performance.

It is naive to believe that you only need to offer large, direct, EVA-incentive bonuses to all employees, and your stock price will skyrocket. The problem is that most employees are unusually risk-averse, and that becomes increasingly true as you work your way down to the shop floor. If the firm does not offer a substantial premium for bearing that risk, retaining employees will be a real issue. The employees will expect a higher average level of pay, or a compensating differential. To the extent that risk is placed more in the control of employees who have the greatest ability to understand and manage such risks, the compensating differential can be reduced without incurring an excessive risk of losing employees.

In practice, most firms have assigned substantial capital spending decision rights to senior executives, and almost none to shop-floor employees. But some elements of the production process are well within the control of shop-floor workers, and, if well managed, they can contribute significantly to creating EVA. These "value drivers" include: productivity improvement, scrap reduction, work-in-process inventory reduction, and reduction of cycle time. All are measurable and are, at least to some extent, within the control of shop-floor employees.

This discussion suggests the representation of optimal EVA measurement and incentive architecture shown in Figure 3.2.

This representation is based on the traditional assignment of capital expenditure decision rights at various levels in the corporation. A significant corporate program of EVA shop-floor training and the involvement of shop-floor employees in EVA-based teams with capital decision rights would allow a rightward shift in the axis (as represented by the dotted line in Figure 3.2).

Briggs & Stratton has allowed significantly different direct EVA value-driver equations in various divisions, with rather interesting results. At one end of the spectrum, its Ravenna, Michigan, castings plant (since sold to MTI) used a largely direct EVA approach (80 percent of the total incentive bonus) with great success. The company believes that plant operation has been successful because of concerted efforts to "shift the axis to the right." As we describe in detail in Chapter 6, it was a relatively small operation (never more than 150 employees), so the efforts of individuals could be readily observed in the plant's EVA performance. Participatory management was the credo from day one, and there was an effective training program for new members of the workforce.

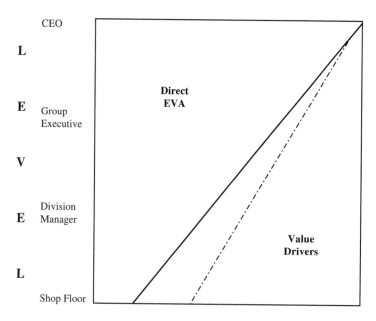

Figure 3.2   Direct EVA versus Value-Driver Measurement and Incentives

At the other end of the spectrum is the company's small-engine division, which has produced excellent EVA results with a single value driver: an incentive system for hourly employees, based on a consistent measure of productivity. The division is extremely large, and its product is highly seasonal and very much subjected to the constraints imposed by its mass-market customers. Because key decision makers in the division are provided with direct EVA incentives, the risk of achieving productivity improvements at the expense of capital discipline is greatly reduced. Hybrid approaches implemented in other divisions have met with mixed results.

It is, of course, easier to outline the principles of corporate strategy and organization than to put them into practice. A heroic effort is often necessary to overcome the innate conservatism of long-time incumbents, with their reflexive resistance to change and fierce defense of bureaucratic satrapies. But, in time of crisis, a new strategy or a renewed commitment to an old one is often the only thing that can revive a company and offer any hope of creating shareholder value, let alone creating value for the other "stakeholders" who have a subordinate claim on a corporation: employees, customers, suppliers, and the community. We next turn to the matter of creating value for all participants—nothing less than the Road Map to Value Creation.

Chapter 4

The Road Map to Value Creation

We now enter a highly contentious area: how to create value not only for shareholders but for the other corporate constituencies or "stakeholders"—employees, customers, suppliers, and the communities in which the corporation is located. The argument is between those who insist that increasing shareholder value is the only target for a company to aim at (pointing out that the other stakeholders will inevitably benefit if the corporation is successful) and others who argue that the corporation must carefully weigh the interests of *all* stakeholders in every major decision. Indeed, some champions of this capacious view seem to argue that the outsiders have equal claim, with shareholders, to the resources of the corporation.

It is notable, however, that no one suggests that the stakeholders have a greater claim than shareholders. And for very good reason: the shareholders provide the *sine qua non* of any enterprise—the capital. They will not fund companies for which there are no expectations of an adequate return (at least equal to, if not greater than, the cost of capital). They will also withhold new capital from failing companies unless there seems to be a realistic prospect of a turn-around, so that, at least on new investment, the expected return is equal to the cost of capital.

Our view, of course, is that the shareholder comes first. It is an inescapable fact of life in a capitalist society. (In a putative socialist society, the state would come first, for it would be the capital provider.) This simple assertion, however, constitutes a public rela-tions problem for many corporations, which accounts for much of the windy and obfuscating rhetoric about stakeholder interests. Corporate embarrassment is most acute when a company is engaged in difficult labor negotiations or when it wants to shift operations to a lower-cost region or to a foreign country.

The outcry is muted if the company is losing money, but if the rationale for the decision to relocate is the need to maintain an ad-equate rate of return, all hell can break loose. And for two good rea-sons: relatively few people understand the financial mainsprings of a business, and for the employees and communities involved, there is real loss. It is not very helpful to tell a worker who has been given a pink slip to read Schumpeter on the "creative destruction" inherent in capitalism. (On the other hand, some companies do offer dis-placed workers an opportunity to transfer to relocated factories.)

Thus, there is no question that short-run conflicts of interest exist between shareholders and other stakeholders—and not only in the case of displaced workers or communities that suffer a diminished tax base and less trade on Main Street when a big factory leaves town. And, on the same point: consumers hardly whoop with joy when the airlines raise prices, happy in the thought that these go-liaths may finally be creating some value for their shareholders.

In the long run, however, there is a mutuality of interest be-tween shareholders and the other stakeholders. A company cannot prosper over an extended period if it has dreadful labor relations, if its products or service are undependable, if its relations with suppli-ers are fractious, if it pollutes the environment, or otherwise makes itself unpopular with the community.

That's putting it negatively—only to emphasize what should be axiomatic. Expressed more positively: a company will enhance shareholder value if it undertakes creative initiatives to foster the well-being of its employees, if it works in close harness with its suppliers and cultivates their loyalty, if it knows its customers intimately and takes pains to meet their specific needs, and if it wins a reputation in the community as a good corporate citizen. In the long run, there is a harmony of interest between the shareholders and the other stakeholders. The old Marxists would call this class collaboration as counterposed to class struggle. It definitely is class collaboration, and it lies deep in the fabric of American capitalism. Or, in terms of game theory, we have a win–win situation, not a zero-sum game. The sums can get larger with mutual cooperation.

This relationship was most cleverly framed by Harry V. Quadracci, founder and owner of Quad/Graphics, one of the leading printers in the United States, at one of the company's holiday dinner dances for employees. A visionary and colorful leader, Quadracci is well known for these outrageously scripted theme galas. At one affair with a circus theme, in the early 1980s, Harry rode in on an elephant, the vice presidents paraded around dressed as clowns, and the corporate secretary was shot out of a cannon, after which Harry settled in to deliver the corporate message: "For each and every one of our partners [i.e., employees], we have $74,000 of capital, mostly debt. The people who gave us the capital demand a 13 percent return. So we must each earn $9,620 for these folks before we can earn a dollar for ourselves." The rest of the speech described to the employees exactly what it would take to meet that challenge.

The goal of top managers is not only to increase shareholder value, but to align shareholders' interests with those of the other stakeholders. All toward the end of creating value—that is, maximizing the amount of total wealth—for all groups involved. This is the goal that forward-looking companies have increasingly embraced after decades of indifference.

In the past, the split between ownership and management that Berle and Means analyzed back in the 1930s had led not only to a slighting of shareholder interests but, understandably, to the neglect of the other stakeholders by managers largely concerned with their own self-interest. Rather than trying to increase value, these managers merely arbitrated value demands among their constituencies. They "bought" labor peace by giving in to uncompetitive labor contracts. They granted price reductions to customers without co-operative price reduction initiatives. They became unresponsive to their customers. They did not manage and reward their employees for productivity gains. Many companies engaged in ill-conceived diversification with the dubious goal of smoothing or "managing" earnings. Others overinvested—or at least put off necessary cut-backs—when the capital might better have been returned to share-holders. Rather than increase value across the board, many companies showed a managerial propensity to redistribute existing value. As a consequence, total value eventually fell.

How can value be increased for all groups concerned? The management imperative will be different for every organization. It will depend largely on the company's distinctive competitive position, its proprietary capabilities, and its internal operational challenges. Yet there is a common thread in the approaches to these challenges that have been taken by most successful value-creating companies. We have attempted to capture this thread in a framework that we refer to as a holistic model of managing for value creation.

We have developed and refined this model over the past few years, for a number of reasons. In the wake of the significant media coverage of EVA, we have received numerous inquiries about how to integrate EVA into an organization. We also want to address the commonly heard criticism that EVA-based management is not sufficiently "strategic" to serve as the primary foundation for good management practices. As a financial measurement and management system, EVA is in itself agnostic on a range of corporate issues. It does not dispute the fact that strategic and organizational issues are important, but it is agnostic in the sense that, rather than prescribe, say, a single best method for inventory management or dictate an overall strategic approach, it encourages managers to entertain all promising possibilities. The EVA discipline furnishes a clear and simple objective—to produce continuous, sustainable increases in EVA—along with a powerful set of incentives to motivate management as well as lower-level employees, as far down as the shop floor.

A final reason for developing a comprehensive model for value creation is that such a model enables a company to communicate to employees and other stakeholders precisely what it takes to create value.

Our holistic model of Managing for Value Creation, devised at Briggs & Stratton, is presented graphically in Figure 4.1.

To create the greatest possible value for shareholders, a firm's top management—and, ideally, everybody down the line—should

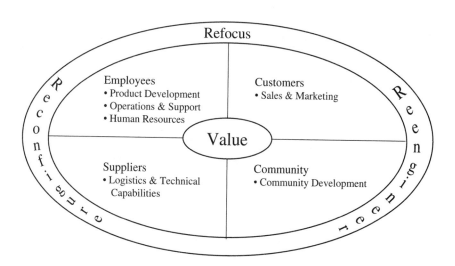

Figure 4.1   **Briggs & Stratton Model: Managing for Value Creation**

be dedicated to creating value in the firm's varied relationships with employees, customers, suppliers, and the communities concerned. These four constituencies should become the focus of imaginative effort by all involved.

The functions associated with each group are set forth in the model. The most important functions—those that integrate employees into the value-creating process—are new product development, operations and support, and development of human resources. Although perhaps the most neglected function in many organizations, human resources development may well have the greatest potential for adding hidden or untapped value. Its aim is nothing less than inspiring and motivating all employees to achieve the ultimate goals of the organization. We believe that all employees possess value-enhancing energy. Management's challenge is to provide an environment in which employees find it in their own interest to release this energy on behalf of wealth creation.

As we move across the model, we see that the function that drives customer value comprises sales and marketing. The keys to value-adding supplier relationships are logistics and technical capabilities. Community development consists, for the most part, in working out cooperative arrangements between the local political entity and the enterprise. Such arrangements, which can take the form of tax incentives, financing support, land development, or other assistance, are what drive value in our mutually beneficial relationships. The community, in turn, gets jobs, an enlarged tax base, and an income stream that reaches the local diner and drugstore.

In reviewing this integrated model, it is important to resist associating any of these functions with specific corporate departments. This is old-fashioned distributive thinking—distributive in the sense of simply dividing up the existing pie, not trying to enlarge it—and it is the kind of approach that an EVA mentality attempts to replace. For example, all corporate managers ought to help promote the human resources goal of motivating rank-and-file employees to create value. And we should all play a sales and marketing role to ensure customer satisfaction, thereby creating value for both buyer and seller.

A few years after refocusing the strategy of Briggs & Stratton and installing an EVA program, management received comments from employees in this vein: "We understand many of the reasons for our success, and we are sure that management has a vision that somehow ties into the concept of EVA. But that vision has not been clearly communicated to us." In response to such comments, management decided to extend the value creation model in such a way that it would identify key methodologies for creating value. They were grouped into three basic categories: (1) strategies, (2) structures and systems, and (3) designs and processes. The result was the development of a one-page "Road Map to Value Creation." Figure 4.2 shows the basic form without any specific content.

The road map provides employees with important insights into how the company's various value-creating initiatives fit together. By viewing the model vertically, each employee can see how the firm intends to create value in his or her own primary functional area. For each function, the map describes the underlying strategy, the supporting structures and systems, and the key designs and processes. By viewing the model horizontally, employees can see how the company's strategies, structures and systems, as well as its designs and processes are integrated along functional lines.

Preparing the road map can be a valuable exercise for organizations that choose to make the effort. It requires not only a commitment to a particular value discipline and its corresponding strategies, but also an identification of key supporting initiatives. Here we draw on the observations on organizational architecture and the "value discipline" of Treacy and Wiersema, discussed in Chapter 3.

Given the development of viable strategies as integral to the proper choice of value discipline, the bottom two rows of boxes in the road map must identify structures, systems, designs, and processes that are consistent with those strategies. Some broad

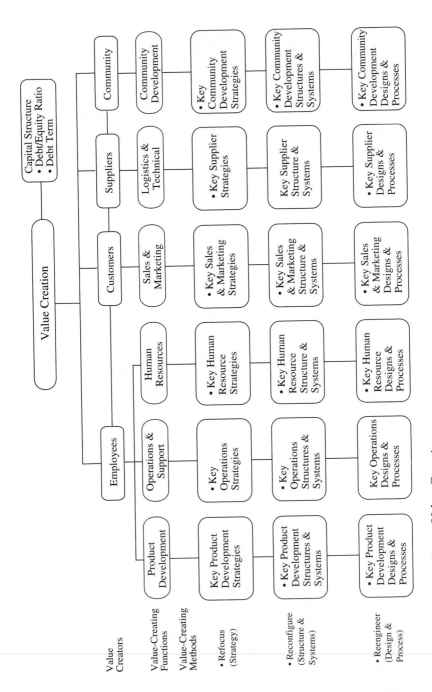

Figure 4.2 Road Map to Value Creation

58

observations on those supporting elements follow. They are identified by reference to the relevant value discipline.

Reconfiguration of Structures and Systems

Cost Leadership

- Organizations that tend to be functional; for large and more complex organizations, decentralized with functionally organized divisions and product-focused operations.
- Systems designed to support highly controlled, reliably repeatable, and cost-effective operations.

Product Leadership

- Generally, flexible decentralized organizations divided along product lines or product groups.
- Systems designed to support and encourage product innovations and successful commercialization of new products.

Best Total Solution

- Organizations most likely segmented along geographic, customer, or industry groups in order to best identify and satisfy individual customer needs; decentralized decision making designed to place power in the individuals dealing directly with customers.
- Systems designed to provide information required to target unique customer preferences and reward employees who best cultivate those customers.

Reengineering of Designs and Processes

Cost Leadership

- Products designed for manufacturability; plants with "hardwired" design for efficient, high-volume production.

- Processes designed to develop low-cost, high-value products and deliver them efficiently to a value-conscious marketplace.

Product Leadership

- Products designed for unique features and maximum performance; plant designs featuring flexible machinery.
- Processes designed to develop differentiated, innovative, and high-featured products, and to cultivate upscale markets.

Best Total Solution

- Products designed to be adaptable to a broad range of customer needs; plants designed for manufacturing of customized product.
- Processes designed to develop a range of unique solutions to support relationship managers.

As the road map is formulated, it is important to identify, much more specifically than set forth above, the actual key elements supporting the choice of value discipline, but these descriptions should offer some direction.

Perhaps one of the greatest shortcomings of modern management is the "plug in" mentality—the concept that any good idea can be plugged into your organization with positive results. This is the case where a manager attends a Tom Peters-type seminar, hears about another firm's adoption of a unique initiative that delivers a positive customer, supplier, or employee response, and returns home all lathered up to try to plug some aspect of the initiative into his or her organization. The manager, for example, may be impressed with an innovation of a small-time grocer who developed a system and process that uniquely identify the fruit and vegetable preferences of customers, is supported by a creative at-home delivery service, and has parlayed the initiative into a billion-dollar business. The manager implements elements of the grocer's idea in his own firm, a producer of high-volume automotive components, and the results are disastrous.

Enduring the discipline of preparing a road map to value creation provides a one-page look at the consistency of strategy across function, and elemental support of strategy. It should then be more difficult to make the mistake of plugging in a best-total-solution type of process, for example, into the strategic architecture of a cost leader.

There is currently developing a burgeoning cottage industry in "best practices" consulting. The consultants will rarely observe (at least in front of a client) that one person's best practice could be another person's strategic nightmare. Again, any organizational element, including a best practice initiative, must be tested for consistency with the chosen value discipline.

We have seen many examples of "excellent companies" that deliver superior value to their customers, suppliers, employees, or communities, and, at the same time, significantly underperform the average company in the S&P 500 or other relevant index, in terms of Market Value Added. The culprit is most likely an inadequate commitment to a value discipline, or a choice of supporting elements that are inconsistent with the value discipline. As we have previously stated, strategy is, at heart, relationship management. Cost leaders, product leaders, and best-total-solution providers all have different relationships with customers, employers, suppliers, and the communities in which they operate. A properly designed EVA program can help identify the areas of relationship management where value is being created or squandered.

Skeptics, of course, may be inclined to side with old-fashioned, authoritarian management types and dismiss the "vision thing" as a chimera. But we maintain that creating and effectively communicating a shared vision serves at least one essential corporate function: it communicates to all managers and employees that the company cannot prosper unless their own actions serve to develop high-value relationships.

We would note in passing that the road map shows that value can also be created by managing the firm's capital structure (see Figure 4.2, box at top right). This is largely a CFO's prerogative, and because employees in general will have little impact on it (other than perhaps incessant pleas to the CFO to manage down the cost of capital), it is not particularly relevant to the issues that lower-ranking employees can have an impact on.

Let us now focus on a Briggs & Stratton customized version of the Road Map to Value Creation—this time, with identification of the specific initiatives that create value (Figure 4.3).

Because a significant portion of the value created at Briggs & Stratton in the past few years has related to operational initiatives, we will concentrate on the Operations and Support section of the road map and provide a more detailed description of the relevant methodologies.

As described in Chapter 3, the cornerstone of Briggs & Stratton's refocused strategy was to restore its competitive position as the broad-scope, low-cost leader in the industry. Given its resources in human and physical capital, as well as its facilities and culture, this was the only strategy that was available to the company and had a reasonable prospect of success. As also discussed earlier, cost leadership is a strategy with well-defined tactics, such as employing high-volume capital equipment, product standardization, continuous cost and quality improvement, and superior process engineering skills. It also requires a decentralized organization—one that places accountability in operating units. When effectively implemented, such tactics can result in an actual cost position at or near the best in the industry.

Figure 4.3 traces the unfolding strategies, as the vertical column under Employees: Operations & Support indicates. The goal

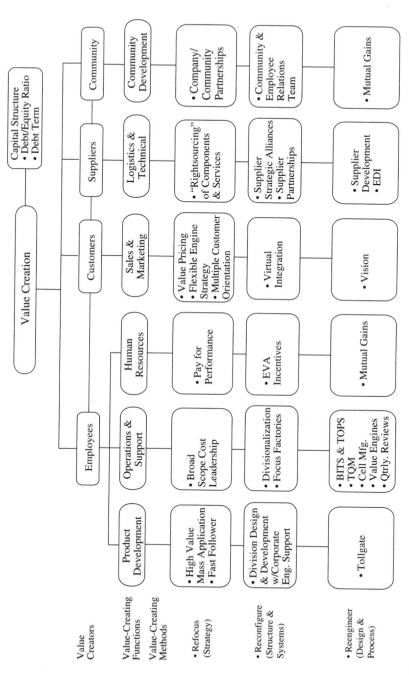

Figure 4.3 Briggs & Stratton Customized Road Map to Value Creation

63

of low-cost leadership leads to decentralization and focus factories, which are in turn supported by BIT, TOPS, TCM, cell manufacturing, value engines, and quarterly EVA reviews—all shorthand for significant innovations. TQM, of course, is Total Quality Management, defined by one of its gurus as "the integration of corporate initiatives into a systematic quality improvement process." Cell manufacturing involves fabrication of engines or subassemblies by groups of workers organized into teams that do the whole job. Each worker is responsible for multiple tasks—in contrast to assembly-line production, where every worker does one or two repetitive tasks hundreds of times a day. Cell manufacturing has been found to increase productivity—largely, because it provides job satisfaction that is totally lacking on an assembly line.

A focus factory, an operation employing 500 to 800 workers, is devoted to only one or two products. This concentration of effort enhances efficiency and lowers costs. Another cost saver is the so-called value engine. It was developed with standardized specifications that would meet the needs of a broad customer base, avoiding most of the spec variations that customers would normally ask for.

The acronyms BIT (Business Improvement Teams) and TOPS (Team-Oriented Problem Solving) involve an especially vital function—the enlistment of shop-floor volunteers to research improvements in the production process. It is undoubtedly the most important aspect of the participatory management style and probably the most fertile area of reengineering at Briggs since its reorganization. The most notable of these initiatives have been the BIT teams launched by Dick Fotsch (then General Manager of the small-engine division), which produce the majority of the engines found on the walk-behind lawn mowers on the market today. (TOPS operates in the large-engine division.)

The BIT initiative was driven by a number of competitive and operational imperatives. As the market shifted from small dealers to mass retailers, the division could not pass on inflationary price increases; thus, cost reduction became critical. Its traditional functional approach to problem solving was replaced by a new focus on continuing quality improvement, with its emphasis on understanding and strengthening the linkage between product attributes and customer preferences.

The small-engine division now operates according to the premise that the people who do the work are those best qualified to improve their work processes. The role of management is to furnish team members with the information needed to develop an understanding of what improvements are required, and of the resources, authority, and responsibility that will enable them to carry out those improvements. The key enablers in successful team reengineering are information technology, customer orientation, and access to resources and direction. Arriving at an understanding of how the process to be improved fits into the business plan is essential.

The BIT program works in this fashion: the small-engine division has five functional departments; among them are die casting, aluminum machining, and ferrous metal machining. Eight business improvement teams, made up of volunteers, were created; all of the teams worked across departmental lines. Thus, if the problem to be researched involves, say, connecting rods—the aluminum rods between the crankshaft and the piston—the BIT team will include a member from the aluminum machining, die casting, subassembly, and final assembly departments.

The overlay of the BIT structure on the functional organization led to a radical change in the workforce's ways of thinking and behaving. Traditional barriers to process improvement came down. Rather than just improving their areas, employees became concerned with improving the total product through improvement of the process that produces it. For example, it was no longer important to have the lowest die cast cost or machining cost. What became important was having the lowest product cost with the highest quality.

To evaluate the progress of the BIT teams in improving efficiency, key measures like process and changeover time were established and reported in quarterly accountability reviews. And such changes did not take long to produce detectable results. During the year before the introduction of BIT, 73 process changes were implemented in the small-engine division. In the first year of BIT, there were 587 process changes, and overall productivity increased by 9 percent.

As impressive as these gains were, the B&S experience with process engineering leads us to offer the following qualification. Fundamental process reengineering is capable, in some cases, of producing very large transformations with enormous benefits (or at least these are the tales that some reengineering advocates prefer to tell), but the real benefits for most companies are those that come from the hundreds of modest process improvements that can be achieved by a properly focused and well-motivated workforce.

Also critical to the company's success was a new EVA Strategic Review process. To fortify its commitment to managing for value creation, the company sponsors periodic (at least quarterly) EVA reviews that bring together the management groups from all the operating divisions and corporate departments. These managers are required to report their EVA results for the prior period and to explain any mid-course corrections in their EVA-based strategic plans.

They are also required, once a year, to update their plans, including their five-year projection of expected EVA results. All the plans are presented at the periodic reviews; the various divisions are put on an annual rotation for plan updates. One or two divisions are featured in each review. The benefits of these periodic forums are significant:

1. Value Discipline and Motivation: division managers must periodically review the status of their EVA initiatives and report results to their peers.

2. Updating of Value-Based Strategic Plans: division managers must also periodically update their plans for changed assumptions, and modify unsuccessful strategies and tactics.

3. Value Forum: the reviews serve as forums for the exchange of relevant ideas among the divisions.

4. Value Insights for Corporate Management: corporate managers get useful insights on where and how value is being created in the organization. It is particularly helpful to schedule these forums just before quarterly board meetings. The CEO can then approach each board meeting with fresh information.

That's a brief review of the Operations and Support section of Briggs & Stratton's Road Map to Value Creation. The sections relating to customers and suppliers can be treated in tandem and are more self-explanatory. The essential point in dealing with these stakeholders is the integration of the selling or buying functions with the needs of customers and buyers. It is self-evident that value is created for both sides in any commercial transaction, unless it occurs under duress or as a result of fraud. But to talk of value in these terms once again reflects what we have called "distributive thinking"—cutting up the existing pie. The problem is how to produce a bigger pie—how to create more value for all concerned.

The technique requires getting more intimately involved with both customers and suppliers. Every successful salesperson knows how to cultivate customers and cater to their needs, but this requires technical expertise as well as a willingness to go the extra mile and adapt the product to the particular requirements of the buyer. This may mean modifying the specifications as necessary, insuring on-time delivery, perhaps crating the product in such a fashion that it can go quickly onto the production line of the customer. Salespeople for surgical devices spend a lot of time instructing doctors and are often present in operating rooms, to observe how a device is being used. With one large customer, Briggs & Stratton stations a permanent representative on the premises, the better to liaise with the B&S home office.

A comparable intimacy exists in the best relationships with suppliers. Teams from both sides normally collaborate on specifications. In "just-in-time manufacturing," suppliers sometimes take over the inventory function of their customers by furnishing product as needed, without waiting for specific orders. The goal for each side is to be as close as possible to the other's organization without formally being a part of it. The value payoff is a product that delivers greater satisfaction to a customer at lower cost and with reduced capital requirements.

A company's relationship with the community often involves a complex interplay of interests that, at best, emerges as a partnership. Hundreds if not thousands of communities solicit companies, offering tax breaks and zoning variances and the promise of an abundant labor supply. Similar concessions are often offered by communities to avert the flight of large employers. New York City has been particularly energetic with these inducements. But the best relationships can perhaps be seen in smaller communities. Briggs & Stratton has had successful experiences locating in small towns, mostly in the South, that have colleges. The towns have generally made some tax concessions, and B&S not only produces jobs for the regular local workforce but, in its peak season, employs college students on its second shifts. Everybody gains.

Quantifying the value accruing to a company's varied stakeholders can be difficult, however—except in the case of employees and shareholders. College students in Murray, Kentucky, will earn much more working at Briggs than at Burger King. Full-time employees anywhere can calculate how much more they are making above the median community wage. Workers receiving an EVA bonus can figure out the incremental value they have received. The enhanced value enjoyed by customers and suppliers as a consequence of integrated relationships is not as easily measured in aggregate, but it can be demonstrated on many fronts: improved sales from more functional and higher-quality products, reduced outlays from cooperative cost reduction initiatives, and reduced capital requirements from joint process and inventory management efforts.

There is no problem, of course, in calculating increases in shareholder value. But, in some quarters, the very concept is under intermittent attack. Much of the rhetoric arises in the context of the turnaround of a corporation that has been managed in a way that destroys value. Often, the change agent is vilified with a name like "Neutron Jack." Part of the problem is the term *shareholder value* itself, which implies to some that the sole corporate goal is to enrich shareholders. Quite the contrary. But it is necessarily the first corporate goal, the achievement of which benefits all the stakeholders. If the shareholders are not enriched, everybody dependent on the corporation will ultimately lose.

To increase shareholder value in the long run, management must engage all the corporate stakeholders in mutually beneficial relationships. There are obligations on all sides: employees must contribute to the value creation effort in order to increase their compensation; customers must support a virtual integration relationship in order for the company to deliver the most value to them; and suppliers must be active participants in efforts to reduce total cost and capital in the supply chain in order to earn the value awarded to them. If these mutually reinforcing relations are achieved, the company will be more likely to deliver to its shareholders a return greater than their cost of capital—in our terms, it will show a positive EVA.

An addendum to the argument should be noted. It is obviously a mistake to regard shareholders and employees as mutually exclusive groups, given the huge increase in private pension funding in recent decades. In 1965, only 16.2 percent of the stock of American companies was owned by institutional investors; by 1999, the figure was nearly 57.6 percent. The institutions were pension trusts, mutual funds, and others providing retirement security to millions of working people. To fulfill their mission, these funds must earn at least a minimum cost-of-capital return. Not only rentiers are concerned with increasing shareholder value.

Konosuke Matsushita, one of the most incisive entrepreneurs of the twentieth century, the creator of one of the world's leading consumer brands (Panasonic) and of hundreds of thousands of jobs, probably said it best some decades ago: "If we cannot make a profit, that means we are committing a sort of crime against society. We take society's capital, we take their people, we take their materials; yet without a good profit, we are using precious resources that could be better used elsewhere."

Chapter 5

The Changes Wrought by EVA

Most companies—by no means all—come to EVA because they have problems. Some are in deep trouble. Some, of course, are doing well but want to improve their performance. Usually, however, distress signals are flying when the company is first attracted to EVA. For example:

- Back in 1994–95, Herman Miller was visibly ailing. The celebrated office furniture manufacturer, headquartered in Zeeland, Michigan, had suffered its first loss in years in 1992. It then returned modestly to the black, but had rapid changes in top management, with three CEOs in six years. When Mike Volkema, the incumbent, got the job in 1995, he took over a company in considerable disarray, with too many executives reporting to the CEO, little capital discipline at the center, and operating expenses that had gotten out of hand.

  Listen to Brian Walker, who was suddenly made CFO at age 33 in 1995: "Our culture was dominated by the idea people, not implementers. You had all those 30 guys who report to the CEO. They'd all say, 'Here's my new idea,' so he'd say

'Great idea!' and they'd go off and do it. I liken it to a football team. Did you ever play touch football when you were a kid and you'd say, 'Everybody out for a pass and I'll see whoever's open?' That's sort of my analogy here. Everybody would go out but nobody was doing the basic blocking and fundamentals. And so when you look at the years '94–'95, while our sales were racing up, our operating expenses were racing up even faster; the amount of capital we were spending was racing up. Every consultant known to mankind was in the building because there wasn't a formal way to make trade-offs."

The trade-offs came after Herman Miller adopted EVA, for which it contracted in January 1996. A year later, the company began to prosper. At the end of fiscal 1998, it could boast in its annual report of record sales ($1.7 billion), record profits ($128.3 million), record EVA ($78.4 million—an improvement of nearly $70 million in only two years). Miller's share price was equally buoyant—surging from $7.72 (adjusted for two stock splits) at the end of fiscal 1996 to $27.69 two years later.

- When Fred M. Butler became CEO of The Manitowoc Company late in 1990, he confronted a classic case of corporate malaise not untypical of a "mature" enterprise. Earnings were falling and there seemed no prospect of a substantial upswing. Growth was only a vagrant dream. Recalled Butler: "I got reports from my major unit managers that essentially said that 'There's no market growth in any of our products or any of our companies for the rest of the decade' and 'We think we are operating efficiently in all of our locations,' which of course they would say. No market growth, no efficiency improvements—that didn't leave much room to do anything."

Not long after, Robert R. Friedl, now Manitowoc's senior vice president and CFO, heard a talk in Milwaukee on a new financial management system called EVA. He was intrigued and talked to Butler, who was desperate to try a new approach. Butler instituted an EVA program and, over the next six years, revived his sluggish company and expanded into new areas. Manitowoc's EVA went from a negative $12 million in 1993 to positive territory in 1995, and it topped $30 million in 1998. In the summer of 1998, Butler retired and was succeeded by Terry Growcock, an enthusiast for EVA since he joined the company in 1994. Under his leadership, its EVA score reached $41 million in 1999.

- International Multifoods, a diversified food company based in Wayzata, Minnesota, was in an equally dismaying state when Gary E. Costley was installed as CEO in January 1997. "The company was a mess," says a caustic Costley, whose expertise in the food business came from a long career at the Kellogg cereal company before he became a business school dean. "It had been described by an analyst as being the longest-running work in progress in the food industry. It went from strategy to strategy to strategy." Founded around the turn of the twentieth century, it had once been big in milling wheat, then had a checkered career manufacturing consumer goods, then switched to being a distributor of other companies' food products, with such sidelines as exporting chicken parts to Russia.

The mess was financial as well as strategic. "The balance sheet was a disaster," says Costley. "They ran the company exclusively for operating earnings. The capital was out of sight; working capital was going up at a phenomenal rate." All of which led Costley, who had long been committed to value-based management, to insist that the board approve an EVA program as a condition of his taking the job. The directors agreed. Two months later, in March 1997, he was joined by William Trubeck as CFO. Trubeck, who occupied the post until March 2000, had held the same job at SPX and had much to do with its conversion to EVA. In two years, the pair turned the company around, but even before that, the stock, which had been dawdling around $15 in 1996, added $3 when Costley was appointed, went to $21 when Trubeck came aboard, rose to the mid-$20s later in the spring when its adoption of EVA was announced, and peaked at $32.

The question before us is: how are such turnarounds engineered—how does EVA work its magic? It is magic without a mystery. Essentially, an EVA program is three things: a measurement system to keep score, an incentive system to make employees partners with shareholders, and a system of financial management that allocates capital in a logical economic framework. In measuring performance, EVA's key ingredient is the capital charge—the cost of the capital invested in a company, in a division, in a branch store, in a product. And capital, of course, includes equity as well as debt; equity does not ride free. As described in Chapter 2, you derive EVA by deducting the capital charge from NOPAT (net operating profit after tax—and after adjusting accounting numbers to reflect economic reality).

EVA will grow if NOPAT increases, either through a cut in operating expenses or a rise in gross revenues that is greater than an increase in expenses. EVA will also rise if there is a decline in the use of capital. At Herman Miller, the EVA training program stresses the "60/11 rule"—an expense dollar saved means a 60-cent increase in EVA (figuring that the effective corporate tax rate is 40 percent), while a dollar in capital saved will boost EVA by 11 cents (since the company estimates its cost of capital is 11 percent). These are the gains that come from curbing profligacy, often necessary when a company first embarks on an EVA program. But over the long haul, EVA growth comes from doing more business—either expanding existing operations or acquiring new ones, all with appropriate capital discipline. EVA analysis becomes an integral part of all decisions about capital expenditures, acquisitions, divestitures, as well as debt-equity ratios.

And driving this focus—motivating it, reinforcing it—is the EVA incentive system, which links employees' bonuses to increases in EVA. Thus, managers have a personal pecuniary interest parallel to that of shareholders, who can anticipate a rise in share prices flowing from a rise in true economic profit. (Chapter 2 described the link between Market Value Added and EVA.)

EVA works its magic through a series of corporate initiatives—some prosaic, some dramatic, and all designed to reorient the corporate ship in the direction of true economic profit. Take the question of hemorrhaging working capital, an affliction that was debilitating International Multifoods, Manitowoc, and many other companies newly embarked on EVA programs. When Costley and Trubeck took over Multifoods, they found that the fastest growing contributor to their operating profits was the export of dark chicken meat to Russia, for which there was an enormous demand. (Russia lacks enough grain to maintain a chicken industry of its own.) But however profitable the chicken trade was on an earnings-per-share basis, "It was an economic disaster from an EVA point of view. It was a classic case," says Costley.

The business just ate up working capital. Each boatload of chicken dispatched from New Orleans sat on the company's balance sheet for six weeks until it was transported and sold. When he deducted the cost of the capital tied up in those drumsticks and thighs—Costley estimated it at a towering 18 percent because of the risks involved—the nominal profits just evaporated. As quickly as he could, he got out of the chicken business, as well as all international trading, which had also included shipping chicken feet to China and used telephone poles to Third World countries.

In the case of Manitowoc, the capital discipline of EVA was what initially attracted CEO Butler. Manitowoc, based in the city of the same name in Wisconsin, is a highly diversified company. It manufactures ice-cube making and refrigeration equipment, it produces cranes for the construction industry, it then owned a shipyard in Sturgeon Bay, Wisconsin (it has since bought two others)—an altogether odd mixture that added to the complexity of monitoring capital flows, for each business had its own wrinkles.

Butler realized that if he could cut back on capital outlays by shedding excess assets and by reducing working capital, the company would not only raise its EVA numbers but be in a position to grow again. After all, EVA improvement boosts not only share price, but also borrowing capacity. It was not a painless process. Most people dislike change—and jobs were lost. Early on, two sister plants that manufactured cranes, in Raynosa, Mexico, and McAllen, Texas, were shut down, and operations shifted to another plant in Georgetown, Texas. In 1995, an even bigger consolidation took place in Manitowoc, where the company's two biggest crane factories were located. Merging them involved an investment of $17 million, but an EVA analysis demonstrated that the savings would offset the cost within two years. At the same time, productivity improvements and outsourcing doubled output, even though the workforce declined from 1,100 to 650.

A corporate-wide campaign was also launched to reduce working capital by slashing inventories and changing sloppy practices in handling accounts receivable and payable. In the company's first two years on EVA, inventories took a big hit—a $50 million reduction, from $84.3 million to $34.2 million. The Sturgeon Bay shipyard shed half a million dollars in excess parts. Manitowoc Ice, the ice-cube-machine company then run by Terry Growcock, was relatively lean, but it had an excessive amount of work-in-process, which Growcock reduced as rapidly as possible. He also instructed his purchasing department to order smaller shipments from suppliers more frequently, thereby producing an additional capital saving.

Even bigger savings came in Manitowoc's large crane company, which initially resisted change. "Ninety-three was when we got our big crane company to listen," says Butler. "We had to bring in a consultant and go through a knock-down, drag-out to get them to actually eliminate the excess inventory that we sold, auctioned, or just scrapped as junk—millions and millions of dollars of it."

Progress was swifter at the ice-cube operation, because of Growcock's commitment. "One of my first jobs at Manitowoc was to take EVA further into Ice," he has said. "At the time, only six managers were on the EVA program, and today, 90 percent of all nonbargaining-unit employees participate. What I did that immediately changed the tenor of the situation was to put supervisors on EVA." Why supervisors? "It made life tougher for them. They had to keep a much closer eye on inventory." They now had a personal stake in the numbers. "Over time, they employed every way that's been invented to keep the flow of materials at the absolute right level so that we didn't have excess costs tied up in inventory."

At other units, it was sometimes difficult to explain the logic of what was going on. The company has a small unit called Manitowoc Remanufacturing that buys, refurbishes, and sells used cranes. The unit would buy a crane for, say, $300,000, then lease it out until it had room in the shop to work on it. The cost of the machine was then reduced by the amount of the rental—say, $100,000—which made it easier to show a profit when the "remanufactured" crane was sold. "The only trouble," says Butler, "was that it was a false earning." The cost of capital tied up in the crane, as well as the other costs incurred in reconditioning it, were not covered by the rent and the nominal profit when the crane was resold. Corporate headquarters—or should we say EVA—imposed more realistic bookkeeping.

Managers who were not alert to the new dispensation got hurt in the pocketbook. Such is the reverse side of EVA incentives, if they fail to motivate appropriate behavior. The Femco subsidiary in Pennsylvania, which manufactures parts to repair cranes, was found to have $800,000 in useless parts in January 1995. Corporate advised Femco to get rid of the inventory as quickly as possible, but the Femco people saw no urgency and did not dispose of it until December. The consequence of carrying $800,000 in unnecessary capital for 12 months was that the unit earned no EVA bonus. Butler resisted all appeals to overlook the "technicality" and allow a bonus. "I said no; the formula was very clear," he recalled.

Throughout the company, the handling of receivables and payables has developed into a fine art. The goal, of course, is to get customers to pay up as soon as possible while delaying payment to suppliers as long as possible. "In previous years, Manitowoc was never concerned about cash," says Greg Matczynski, controller of Manitowoc Cranes. "We just went with vendor terms. Now we have a standard of 45 days." The change was easy to effect; the company has ample clout. An EVA analysis revealed when to take a discount in return for faster payment. Matczynski says the new policy saves the company $80,000 a year.

Manitowoc's marine division has been adept at getting progress payments on big jobs. One job involved building a self-loading barge—a $14 million contract, and Sturgeon Bay's first shipbuilding assignment since 1985; another job was a major barge conversion project worth $10 million. In both cases, monthly progress payments were negotiated, greatly reducing working capital needs. "If we spent $3 million the first month on steel, we got reimbursed immediately," says controller Doug Huff. Manitowoc Cranes has also been able to obtain progress payments from customers for whom it is making specially designed equipment. It gets a 10 percent down payment, plus periodic payments to cover labor and materials as work proceeds. This shifts much of the cost of capital from Manitowoc to the purchaser. Why do buyers agree? In some cases, the amount of money involved is trifling to the buyer, whereas the aggregate savings on many such deals is substantial to Manitowoc.

Reducing working capital has also gotten a lot of attention at Herman Miller, Inc. In its effort to speed the collection of receivables, the SQA subsidiary reduced the average number of days outstanding by 33 percent, from 45 days in 1992 to 30 days in 1997. This was achieved not by hectoring customers to pay up but by concentrating on reliability, for the most common cause of delayed payments is incomplete shipments. If one or two pieces are missing, the customer is likely to refuse to pay until the entire order has arrived—and why not? What would you do?

At the other end of the money spout, purchasing agents have transformed their approach. In the past, says Dave Guy, General Manager, Zeeland Operations, "Our purchasing agents kind of ignored payment terms. They were interested in getting cash discounts, because that would lower materials prices." Their performance was measured by the prices they paid, with no consideration of the capital cost of speedy payments. No longer. As an example, Guy offers an analysis that came from extending payments to three aluminum suppliers. In one case, by taking 30-day terms rather than 15, there was an EVA improvement of $14,174 on a purchase of $3.1 million. In three such examples, involving $6,658,238 in aluminum buys, EVA was boosted by $27,746. Every little bit counts.

Throughout Herman Miller, EVA has brought a new emphasis on lean manufacturing—which means low inventories both of raw materials and finished products. Instead of building up a hoard of office furniture ready to be shipped when orders arrive, the goal is to tailor production to orders as they come in. Touring a visitor around the Zeeland factory a few years ago, Jackson Spidell, then the plant manager, proudly pointed to vast empty areas around the walls that used to be filled, floor to ceiling, with raw materials. Now the shelves had been pulled down. Over the space of one year, capital tied up in inventory was reduced from $8 million to $6.2 million. He pointed to signs around the factory displaying a quotation from Shigeo Shino, a leading advocate of lean manufacturing: "Inventory is like a narcotic—tolerate it and you'll soon slide into a state of addiction and require larger and larger quantities in order to feel secure."

A company can only go so far in improving its inventory controls or fine-tuning its management of receivables and payables. More important in the long run is the mediating role of EVA analysis in every decision involving capital expenditure, whether it's a question of buying a machine, adding floor space, acquiring a new plant or a new business, or shedding an old one.

The new approach to decision making is often grasped quickly, if only because of the link to executive compensation. A homely example of the impact of EVA is offered by David Sussman, the chairman of South Africa's JD Group, a chain of over 500 furniture, appliance, and consumer electronics stores. The group took EVA down to the store level—that is, it measured the EVA performance of each branch store and rewarded the manager accordingly. As Sussman later told an EVA conference, "We have seen an amazing change of culture coming about at this branch manager level. Previously, branch managers were very keen to buy new trucks simply because they were battered. We now find these guys resisting that sort of behavior. They're now telling us, 'Listen, we don't need a new truck. We'd rather refurbish the truck we have. We can get away with it.' Or it makes no sense to refurbish a store. So let's just do a coat of paint, and that's enough. Clearly, there are risks involved in this sort of thing, [but] we believe that the group has the necessary checks and balances. Branch managers cannot reduce the size of the store unless it's in keeping with a format that we've agreed to."

SPX, the fabulously successful diversified manufacturer headquartered in Muskegon, Michigan, has a similar, celebrated story of the wondrous effects of EVA capital constraint that is worth retelling. The executives at Contech, one of SPX's divisions, were mulling over a proposal to buy two robots. The cost was $2 million—

hardly trifling, but the need was urgent. Still, they hesitated. "They thought how much it would affect their compensation," says CEO John Blystone, with a chuckle. An inquiry revealed an alternative: two demonstration models were available. All they needed was a paint job. The manufacturer was willing to give the usual warranty. The price was $1 million and the deal was done.

But there is no need to be cynical. More than personal incentives are involved in these decisions. The EVA analytic model, once it is grasped, often effortlessly reorients thinking and planning. For most people, anyway; we have described exceptions. And the new approach can take hold quickly. In the fall of 1995, a unit of Herman Miller called IMT (Integrated Metal Technology), which makes metal furniture parts, told Brian Walker that it needed a new factory to increase capacity. The conversation occurred before the formal adoption of EVA but when the concepts were being widely discussed among top executives. Walker was sympathetic, though the $4 million cost was hardly insignificant. But, weeks later, the IMT people failed to submit a formal proposal to the Miller board. In the interval, Walker discovered, they had decided on an alternative solution—adopting the Toyota production system, which involved rearranging production facilities to reduce work areas, and also drastically reducing materials inventories to little more than what was needed for a day's production. There was now enough floor space to obviate the need for a new plant.

At Herman Miller, the EVA angle of vision has also transformed the perennial issue of whether to rebuild old equipment or buy new. "In the past," says Matt Campbell, a senior project engineer at the Zeeland plant, "we did a lot of rebuilding of old equipment. We thought this was the cost-effective solution. Looking back, in some cases it would have been better to replace the asset."

He gives two examples. The first involved a boring machine, which worked well mechanically but its computer controls were on the blink. The engineer responsible for the project initially decided that it would be best to replace the machine with a new one costing $325,000, rather than with a control retrofit costing $80,000. A new machine would be nearly 100 percent reliable, whereas the rejuvenated one would be only 90 percent reliable. But when all factors were taken into account, a retrofit turned out to be cheaper. The boring machine operated independently; if it went down, it did not hold up the entire production line. Hence, despite the costs of downtime, it was cheaper to keep the old machine. By contrast, there was the case of the high-speed router. It also needed a retrofit, but it was a bottleneck in the production line. When it stopped functioning, the whole line went down. EVA calculations quickly proved that a new machine, with 100 percent reliability, would be the far cheaper way to go.

Here is a snapshot of how an EVA analysis of a proposed capital outlay works. It comes from Centura Banks, Inc., of Rocky Mount, North Carolina, an aggressive and highly successful one-bank holding company. The question arose a while back as to the desirability of buying or leasing a new PBX system. The purchase price was $134,000, whereas a five-year lease would cost $34,000 annually. The life of the PBX was estimated to be 10 years. Cranked into the calculation was a 15 percent cost of equity capital, an 8.75 percent cost of debt capital, and a marginal tax rate of 44.04 percent. The result was a cumulative present value (PV) of $121,000 for the lease cost, as compared with a cumulative PV of $109,000 for the cost of purchase. Hence the decision to buy.

The question also arose as to the wisdom of adding an express drive-up lane to a branch bank. The total construction and lease cost came to $1.1 million. The annual net operating profit after tax was forecast to rise, over five years, from $32,705 to $67,353. But when the cost of capital was subtracted each year from NOPAT, there was substantial negative EVA in the first two years, after which EVA became positive. Adding up the five years produced a cumulative EVA value of $7,178. Discounted, the net present value (NPV) of EVA stood at zero. When EVA comes in as a wash, the green light flashes, because it means that the rate of return is just sufficient to provide shareholders with adequate compensation for risk taking.

Since 1994, EVA has been a key factor in evaluating proposed acquisitions. Many target banks seemed attractively priced when the major limiting factor for Centura was the amount of share dilution it could prudently sustain. EVA analysis, however, indicated that several candidates were overpriced; it was the cost of capital, of course, that made the difference. In two instances in 1995, however, Centura was able to overcome this problem by persuading the sellers to accept lower prices than other bidders were offering. Centura paid $16.4 million for the Cleveland Federal S&L in Shelby, North Carolina, and $59.4 million for the First Southern S&L in Asheboro, North Carolina. The two banks accepted the lower offers presumably because of their belief in Centura's favorable prospects, inasmuch as the purchase was made in common stock.

Divestitures work the same way as acquisitions. If the S&Ls that Centura bought had been EVA companies—which they were not—they would have gone through a similar exercise, discounting to the present the value of forecasted future EVA and comparing it with the prices that Centura offered. At its core, there is a beguiling simplicity to EVA.

Chapter 6

Extending EVA to the Shop Floor

The scene was a sparsely furnished conference room in the Briggs & Stratton plant in Wauwatosa, Wisconsin. Some 30 people had gathered to hear an "Improvement Team Presentation" by seven rank-and file workers and two supervisors who had grappled with the problem of reducing inventory losses in the Specialty Products Division. Present were several executives, from the plant level to the corporate officers, including CEO Fred Stratton. The team coordinator, a veteran worker named Leo Duehning, presided and got a laugh by stating that it was normal at such sessions to start with a joke—"But I don't know any."

Then he outlined the team's mission: to reduce the division's 1997 inventory loss of $253,000 by 25 percent in the following year. He stressed the costs of inaccuracy—downtime when parts presumably in inventory were not available, and overtime expense when missing parts had to be fabricated quickly. The team found that most of the problems were caused by erroneous counts and over- and underestimates. Typically, parts were weighed in scales, with the count determined by the weight. The difficulty was that nobody knew for sure how much the scales weighed! Part of the solution was to install mechanical counters on production machines. In some operations, "standard loads" were also used—that is, boxes of parts that contained a fixed quantity when full. Obvious reforms, one would think, but they had somehow been overlooked by management.

The changes helped produce more than the targeted 25 percent improvement and indeed totally wiped out the $253,000 inventory loss—all of which gave a healthy boost to the division's EVA. Duehning modestly observed that his colleagues could not take all the credit—other groups had also attacked inventory losses—but he got a big hand.

What was interesting in this exercise was that all the team members were volunteers and all its hourly rated employees were union members. Rank-and-file workers at the Wauwatosa plant (now numbering 1,800) are on an EVA bonus plan negotiated with their union. Briggs & Stratton has been among the leaders in extending EVA to the shop floor, as have Herman Miller, SPX, and Centura Banks.

Indeed, the Briggs & Stratton Wauwatosa operation, with its productivity improvement teams, has become something of a model of union–management cooperation. But a lot of ructions preceded this happy state of affairs—strikes, one debilitating slowdown, a "corporate campaign" against the company, and endless toing and froing with the National Labor Relations Board. Briggs' factories in the Milwaukee suburbs have been organized for decades, much like other Midwest industries that toppled before the great organizing drives of the 1930s and 1940s. Milwaukee was an especially hospitable place for unions; it was unusual among big cities for the long tenure of its socialist mayors, dating back to 1912 and continuing uninterruptedly until 1940, and resuming in the 1950s. Briggs & Stratton's workers were represented for years by the Allied Industrial Workers, an independent union that later merged with the United Paperworkers International Union of the AFL–CIO.

Relations between union and management were reasonably harmonious—or at least not unreasonably contentious—until, in 1983, the local elected a militant slate of officers that was a throwback to an ancient era of unionism imbued with the ethos of class struggle. Arguments grew more heated, what mutual trust had existed evaporated, and the union leaders apparently viewed management as rapacious capitalists bent on sacrificing the well-being of the workforce in pursuit of higher profits.

The climactic clash occurred in 1993–1994, precipitated by a letter sent to the president of the union local by the company in July 1993, proposing negotiations to reach a new agreement by the end of the year. The union was not agreeable to early negotiations, probably anticipating what came next—a company announcement in August that it was planning to restructure operations and create new "focus factories," each of which would be devoted to a single product or related groups of products, in the Milwaukee area. The focus factory initiative represented a $20 million investment to achieve productivity improvements and make Briggs & Stratton's Milwaukee operations more competitive; the company was still climbing out of the slump in which it had found itself in 1989. But setting up the new factories meant new job classifications, reassignment of workers, elimination of a large measure of featherbedding— managerial initiatives that unions invariably find threatening, for such changes undercut the protective shield unions try to offer members.

So the union leadership resisted, vociferously. One official vowed that "We will bring this company to its knees." The weapon chosen was not a strike, which would have been illegal under the existing contract, but a slowdown that was not as patently illegal and went on for weeks, causing the company a multimillion-dollar loss. Late in October 1993, the company tried to get another dialogue going with the union about focus factories and indicated that if there were no agreement, it would relocate some operations outside the Milwaukee area. The union still refused to talk, and the slowdown continued. On November 8, a federal court granted an injunction that ended the slowdown and, a few days later, the company fired three ringleaders. Some months later, an arbitrator finally ruled that management had been within its rights in changing departmental classifications in support of the focus factories. The move "was clearly based on legitimate business considerations," the arbitrator declared.

Meantime, the union had launched a vigorous "corporate campaign" against Briggs & Stratton—essentially, a public relations campaign designed to embarrass the company in the eyes of the community, its shareholders, bankers, and customers. The union's minions assailed Briggs & Stratton at its annual shareholders' meeting, and vainly campaigned to get a dissident on the Briggs board. They also made disruptive appearances at the annual meetings of Banc One and the Wisconsin Energy Corporation, on whose boards CEO Fred Stratton served. They even went so far as to pressure regulators, again in vain, to disapprove the Firstar/First Southwest banking merger, because two Briggs directors sat on the Firstar board.

One of the coups in the corporate campaign against Briggs was a cover story in the December 2, 1994, issue of *National Catholic Reporter* entitled, "Adios American Dream." The NCR is an independent journal of a left liberal persuasion, but the word Catholic in its title can give the impression to untutored readers that in some sense it speaks for the church or at least for a broad stratum of mainstream Catholic opinion. Hence the sting felt by Briggs's leaders from an editorial accompanying the article which declared that they "live in either denial or moral blindness." It denounced layoffs at the Milwaukee plants as "motivated by a new profit-charged management strategy [an apparent reference to the EVA discipline] and the advent of free trade." And a lot more. The company tried to get its account of events printed in the paper, but the editors offered a much shorter version that was unacceptable to the company. In the end, the company sued for libel.

Despite the embarrassment it caused, the corporate campaign eventually faded away as many of its supporters began to understand the ideology and agenda of the campaign's architects. Meantime, the company established four new focus factories away from Milwaukee—in Rolla, Missouri; Auburn, Alabama; Statesboro, Georgia; and Ravenna, Michigan. Distressed by all the turmoil and the loss of jobs in the Milwaukee area, the United Paperworkers International Union, in January 1997, imposed a trusteeship on the Briggs & Stratton local (No. 7232). Its officials were removed, and a trustee was appointed to run its affairs. The labor agreement was reopened, modified, and ratified. It included provisions for employee involvement teams and other initiatives intended to improve the productivity of Milwaukee operations. And when the trusteeship was lifted and elections were held for officers' positions in the local, a more moderate group was elected.

The new leadership of the local wholeheartedly supported productivity teams on the shop floor. As for the company's libel case against the *National Catholic Reporter*, it never came to trial. After it was initiated, the NCR filed a motion to dismiss the action, but, in October 1997, a federal judge rejected it, upholding the company's cause of action. The company viewed this decision as vindicating its position and shortly thereafter dropped its suit.

EVA is now firmly entrenched in Briggs' Wauwatosa plant as the variable component of shop workers' pay. If the company makes its EVA target, workers get a 3 percent bonus based on their wages for the year. The bonus is uncapped; thus, the percentage rises to the extent that the company exceeds the target sum; the bonus could go to 6 percent or higher, though this has not happened yet. At the focus factories in Missouri and the South, incentive pay is based on EVA drivers, such as productivity increases.

At the Wauwatosa plant, the Specialty Products Division has led the way in improvement-team initiatives—and that for an odd historic reason. The division used to be located a dozen miles away, in Menomonee Falls, Wisconsin, a geographic remove that kept the workers relatively shielded from the bitter union–management skirmishes of 1993–1994. Later, in 1996, Briggs sold the plant to Harley Davidson and moved the workers to the Wauwatosa facility, which had been thinned out by the removal of operations to the focus factories. The new arrivals had less of a problem than others in the Wauwatosa plant in embracing union–management cooperation.

The improvement teams have tackled a variety of problems, all of them undramatic, if not downright mundane, but these forays into minutiae are the stuff of productivity gains. One group was formed in Department 770 to reduce the cost of producing tappets—the sliding rods in engines. The department was losing money on many of the tappets; the team discovered that the problem was the excessive thickness of some of the wire used to make the item, which also added to the time that metal had to be heated. By switching to a thinner wire that required less heating, the team projected total annual savings of $221,896.96.

In another area of the factory, assembly of the so-called "quantum mufflers" was too slow, averaging 4,597 assemblies per eight-hour shift in fiscal 1996, with two workers on the job. The goal was to increase output to between 5,800 and 6,400 assemblies per shift with the same workforce. After extensive study by the team, a number of changes in the assembly process were made—such things as adding a roller to the parts washer to avoid jamups, and raising the incline of the conveyer belt coming from the washer, to keep parts from sliding back. Magnets were also affixed to pallets to keep parts from falling off, and a lot more—small improvements that cumulatively had a big impact on efficiency. In the first eight months of fiscal 1998, the average number of units assembled per shift increased to 5,844. After expenditures of $2,425, the team had produced net savings of $37,837.

Another group took on the task of reducing the changeover time needed to ready a metal stamping press to handle a new job, which required a number of adjustments. When the team started studying the problem, it took two workers nearly 22 hours to complete the changeover. After a number of alterations in the process, including moving the press to a better location, the time needed was reduced to an hour and 52 minutes, for an annual saving of $64,659.

Until it was sold in 1999, Briggs' iron casting foundry, in the small town of Ravenna, Michigan, was for four years an interesting experiment in a stand-alone EVA operation. Its bonus for shop-floor workers was totally dependent on the foundry's own results, with no part of it determined by companywide performance—in contrast to the operation in Wauwatosa, where the entire shop-floor bonus is based on total corporate performance. The Ravenna plan was so designed because it was a new start-up in 1995 (the plant was bought from the SPX Corporation and then rebuilt). Its operations were self-contained, and the workforce was small enough (initially 100, later 150) to allow each worker to see the link between personal performance and plant outcome. Around 60 percent of the castings produced at Ravenna were sold to outside customers in the auto industry, with the remaining 40 percent going to other units of Briggs & Stratton.

Workers were recruited locally and were given EVA training from the outset. Competitive wages were offered—workers made between $25,000 and $30,000 a year—with part of the recruiting appeal being the bonus add-on. No union was involved, so the company had more flexibility in designing the plan than at Wauwatosa. The plan provided for a bonus of 6 percent if all targets were met for the year, and proportionately less if there was a shortfall. In the event that targets were exceeded, the bonus could go as high as 12 percent, at which point it was capped.

Multiple targets were part of the plan. The foundry had an EVA improvement target for the year, but that determined only 80 percent of the workers' bonus. The other 20 percent was dependent on achieving goals in three areas—molding efficiency, scrap reduction, and attendance. The efficiency with which castings were made and the reduction of scrap obviously contributed to overall productivity, but the reduction of absenteeism was also important, for a regular employee was generally more efficient than a substitute. The shop-floor workers had complete control over these matters, and progress reports were posted each month. On the other hand, as Ed Bednar, then general manager of the entire castings division, pointed out, "One thing the employees could not solely control was the volatility of some of the markets we serve. We felt it wouldn't be fair to them to have their factor based 100 percent on plant EVA, since the sales dollars could go up or down drastically for reasons outside their control, thus impacting employee motivation and morale." However, achievement of the three goals under direct workers' control could to some extent offset a slump in sales and thus in plant EVA.

The plan also differed from the standard executive bonus plan in that there was no bonus bank. Bednar on that point: "Banking is a good concept for senior level managers . . . however, I think the shop floor employee would not understand the banking concept, and would see it basically as management holding back a bonus they've earned." Not every employer has taken that view, as we will see when we look at the Sirona plan in Germany.

The plan resulted in a high level of worker participation, even though the bonus never reached 6 percent. In fiscal 1997, for example, it came to 1.43 percent, which meant that a worker making $25,000 a year received $375.50—hardly a bonanza but not chicken feed either.

And the specific improvements? Paul Duvendack, plant manager back in 1997–1998, reported several achievements from a "down time task force" that he organized in October 1997. It consisted of representatives of the melt and mold departments—the main production departments—from each of the two shifts that the plant ran, as well as people from maintenance, plus Duvendack. From time to time, one or two foremen sat in, but the task force was basically employee-driven. It met regularly to exchange ideas and to brainstorm vigorously, and it came up with several useful proposals that had not occurred to management.

In the Ravenna foundry, the core operation involved sending iron from the three huge cylindrical furnaces to the molding line. The molten iron was poured from the furnaces into huge ladles, shaped like teapots, each of which contained 4,500 pounds, and the ladles in turn were transported by a monorail hoist near the ceiling to the molding lines, where they were poured into the molds to make the castings. There was a problem, however, when the molding had to stop, perhaps for a pattern change in the mold, or a slowdown. "Communication back to the melt department was somewhat haphazard, with a bunch of hand signals," says Duvendack. If the melt department didn't get the message, the 4,500-pound load would solidify in 15 minutes and had to be thrown away; this happened too frequently. The solution proposed by the task force was to install a stop–go, red-and-green light system to alert the melt department when to send iron. The savings amounted to $3,960 per week—some $200,000 a year.

Duvendack offered some other examples: "Molding machine operators needed to scrape built-up sand out of feed hoppers on their machines once an hour. This amounted to wasted time and effort spent on non-value-added activity. The result of not scraping was a plugged-up hopper, causing 30 to 40 minutes of downtime a week. The task force put polyethylene liners in the sand hoppers. The sand would not stick to them, eliminating the need to scrape the hoppers and the resulting downtime. Savings in excess of $640 a week.

"Bottom pour ladles tend to build up slag and impurities. This accumulation caused problems in pouring. Previously, an entire ladle needed to be cleaned out, requiring 20 minutes of downtime and four people to carry out the process. Instead, we cleaned out the impurities with an oxygen torch, requiring only six minutes. Savings of $1,370 per week."

And lots more.

We now move on to Herman Miller, Inc., a company renowned for many things, not only its Eames lounge chair and its sleek office furniture (Joel Stern's office is entirely populated with HM product) but a dedication to participatory management that goes back several decades and that, in recent years, has been successfully wedded to the EVA discipline.

Herman Miller, headquartered in the small town of Zeeland, Michigan, is notable as well for its beguiling combination of high-mindedness and *joie de vivre*. A reader leafing through HM's 1996 annual report, for example, will encounter a startling vision on page 35—photos of several of the company's senior managers cavorting in hula hoops. CEO Mike Volkema is seen twirling a hoop around his hips, while then CFO Brian Walker is expertly rotating two hoops around his extended arms. The caption explains, "Despite all their responsibilities, they can still let down once in a while. They're pretty good both at balance sheets and hula hoops, the fad of the fifties." Equally surprising is a sentence in red: "After one good year—even a really good year—they have yet to prove themselves over time." (They subsequently did.)

Such irreverence and jocularity are characteristic of the company. Miller is informal, laid back, and insistently egalitarian. Every day is dress-down Friday. A visitor in a suit feels distinctly out of place. More in keeping with the dress code are two executives from a subsidiary who arrive dressed in corduroys, sweaters, and windbreakers, looking as if they had just tumbled out of the cab of a tractor-trailer. In Millerland, no one would dream of addressing a boss by anything but a first name; there are no foremen on the shop floor but instead "work team leaders," and the rank and file are referred to as "employee-owners" (most do own shares). It's all part of the participatory management style, which goes back decades.

Herman Miller's origins were not especially auspicious. It was founded in 1905 when "a group of Zeeland citizens had a defunct canning company on their hands [and] decided that the practical thing to do would be to make furniture in their building," wrote a later CEO, Hugh DePree, in his corporate history, *Business as Unusual*. Furniture, after all, was a manufacturing staple of that section of western Michigan whose largest city was Grand Rapids, which soon became less renowned as a locality than as a synonym for kitsch. The Star Furniture Company was renamed Herman Miller, Inc., in 1923, in tribute to a large shareholder who was the father-in-law of the founder, D.J. DePree. The firm made furniture for the home and was as undistinguished as its contemporaries until it switched from traditional period pieces to modern furniture in the mid-1930s, having been converted to the new gospel by designer Gilbert Rohde. The flavor of the company can be sampled by the comment of Hugh DePree about his father, "D.J.," who was CEO at the time: "D.J. felt there was a kind of dishonesty in copying old pieces and faking finishes to get an Old World antique look."

Modern furniture was not only more honest but it also sold well and had economies of scale. DePree writes: "We had learned that in modern we were delivering more furniture per dollar. We were also sure that good modern design would have longer life, therefore becoming an answer to every manufacturer's dream for repetitive cuttings of the same components." Herman Miller opened a showroom in New York in 1941 and, over a relatively few years, became celebrated for the elegance of its design and the quality of its craftsmanship. After World War II, its new design director, George Nelson, brought in several new designers, including Eames, Alexander Girard, and Isamu Noguchi, among others.

Herman Miller, Inc., was still a small operation with only 120 workers when, in 1950, it enthusiastically embraced the so-called Scanlon Plan, a scheme for labor–management cooperation on the shop floor that would naturally appeal to executives whose ethical sensitivity was offended by the "fakery" of manufacturing period furniture. Both D.J. DePree and his son Hugh had a paternalistic regard for their small workforce, largely made up of longtime

employees, many of the same Dutch Reformed stock who had settled the area a century before. In 1949, both DePrees had attended
a lecture by Dr. Carl Frost, of Michigan State University, on "Enterprise for Everybody." They were instant converts. The plan that
Frost described had originated with a one-time labor leader named
Joseph Scanlon. Its essence was enlisting the continuous participation of the laborforce in the day-to-day operations of a company to
the end of increasing productivity, the benefits of which would be
shared with the workers. The DePrees hired Frost to create such a
plan for their company.

Hugh DePree writes: "We learned through Jack Frost that the
keys to this plan were these: People throughout the organization
have to be individually identified as resources who can accomplish
the objectives of the organization. . . . People then have to have the
opportunity to participate, to question, to initiate, to be innovative. . . . People need equity; therefore, Herman Miller needs an understandable way of sharing the financial benefits that will accrue
through participation.

"And so," DePree continues, "a change began, a change that
was satisfying but irritating, rewarding but frustrating; a change
that brought us all closer together. . . ."

Committees were set up to work on improvements in production and to screen suggestions from the rank-and-file, many of
which were adopted, and the plan became an integral part of the
HM culture, aided by the fact that the bonus averaged 10 percent of
wages for the first 10 years. It remained essentially unaltered until
1979, when a revised plan was put into effect to accommodate the
expansion of the company to many locations outside Zeeland, including Europe. Moreover, the mix of the workforce had changed.
In 1950, 90 percent of the employees in Zeeland were on the factory
floor; now the organization had grown to 2,500 people, many of
whom wore white collars. After much study by a delegate committee representing the rank-and-file, the Scanlon plan was recast.

Goals were established for different segments of the company, and the bonus formulas became more elaborate. Quarterly bonus payments continued.

Then, in 1996, the company adopted a full-blown EVA program, with a traditional incentive bonus plan for top executives. This plan was not regarded as appropriate for shop and office workers. After decades of quarterly bonuses, a year was too long for workers to wait; moreover, quarterly payments showed a more direct link between effort and reward. So the quarterly payments have continued, with the significant difference that they are now based on the same EVA targets as those in the management plan. If the company achieves the expected improvement in EVA, participants get a bonus equal to 7 percent of salary, and more if the goal is exceeded by stipulated sums.

While no longer called the Scanlon Plan, the central concept remains participative management. One oddity of the program is that executives on the traditional EVA incentive plan also receive the quarterly cash bonus, but their participation is limited to $42,900 of their pay. Why the double dipping? "There's a psychological element," says Dave Guy, "We're in this together when we hand out checks. Some areas have ceremonies." Moreover, everybody was included in the old Scanlon plan.

The new EVA quarterly bonus plan got off to a roaring start, producing a payout of over 30 percent for the third quarter of fiscal 1997 and remaining in the double digits thereafter; the high point was 31.3 percent for the fourth quarter of fiscal 1998. The company keeps interest high with monthly reports on the company's EVA progress and periodic workshop meetings, of which more in the next chapter.

EVA has also been brought down to the shop floor in a North Carolina bank that has made the most innovative use of EVA of any bank in the world. Centura Banks, Inc., adopted EVA in 1994 and, from the outset, covered all its employees, who now number nearly

3,500. The three dozen top executives have a standard bonus plan, supplemented by a stock option plan. Salaried employees have a plan that pays a bonus up to 10 percent of their pay, based on the bank's EVA performance. The 500 salespeople have the most ingenious plan of all—an EVA-based commission system. Each salesperson receives a salary and, in addition, can qualify for a bonus determined by his or her "value added." The plan works this way: every product the bank offers—some 56 of them—has a value-added component, established after deducting all the costs allocated to it—including, of course, the cost of capital. Every month, the bank prepares a report that lists the sales of each product and the net value added for each. Each salesperson receives a copy of that report, together with one, in the same format, detailing his or her own monthly performance, with a total for the net value added. Subtracted from the total are salary, fringe benefits, other expenses, and share of overhead. After further adjustments, the bottom line represents the value added. The salesperson collects 10 percent or 12 percent of that sum, depending on how large it is, as an incentive bonus. Paid quarterly, it has become a significant addition to compensation.

While EVA on the shop floor is both practical and effective, it has not yet become a mass movement. Most companies start EVA bonus programs on the executive level, and gradually push it down through the managerial ranks and then to salaried personnel. Hourly related workers tend to be left out, sometimes because of union resistance and, in other cases, because of the inability of management to see the link between EVA incentives and job performance. In this view, workers lack the decision-making power to respond effectively to EVA incentives, but this judgment overlooks the great reservoir of knowledge about the production process that can be tapped if workers participate in EVA.

A question we are often asked is: "How do you negotiate an EVA-based compensation program into an agreement with an organized workforce?" Union leaders have traditionally been instilled with the belief that "fair" means "equal," and that all performance-based compensation should be viewed with suspicion. Moreover, by their nature, unions are adversarial; any negotiating situation is adversarial, even among individuals, at least until a deal is struck, but with unions there is sometimes no deal without a bitter contest. So how are you going to sell unions on an incentive system that is supported by rather sophisticated microeconomic principles?

There are two answers. While conflict is inherent in the bargaining nexus, there is also a tradition of union–management cooperation in the United States and other democratic countries. Many unions have understood that prosperity for their employers—enlarging the pie available for sharing—redounds to the benefit of their flock, and they will cooperate in productivity deals with the boss. The second answer is that management can communicate directly with the workforce. Winning over the rank and file can be the real key to success in promoting EVA on the shop floor. Many companies fail to communicate effectively with their unionized employees because they have been cautioned by legal counsel that such communications may be prohibited. It is true that unilateral discussions of wages, benefits, and other terms of employment are off limits under U.S. labor law, but a broad range of management prerogatives may be discussed directly with employees.

So you can discuss EVA as a performance metric with shop-floor employees. You may train your employees in the basics of EVA and in how to apply the strategies to their work areas. And you can communicate to them periodically the EVA performance of their department, plant, or division, and explain the reasons results were good or bad.

Perhaps the greatest concern of the unionized employee is job security. You should communicate to all employees the obvious fact that if a plant or division cannot be EVA-positive in the long run, it cannot continue to exist. The good old days when companies believed they had the luxury of subsidizing value-killing operations with economically profitable ones are over. At the same time, you owe it to your employees to tell them what steps, however painful, are required to make various operations EVA-positive.

To most union members, the value creation process is a "black box." Seldom are they privy to the company's value discipline, its operating model, and the basic economics of the particular operations they are involved in. They believe they cannot trust management because they do not know what the business is up to—the "next shoe to drop" syndrome. EVA can help to explain decisions that were previously incomprehensible to hourly employees. And as information drives beliefs and beliefs drive behavior, you can begin to create a workforce that will participate in the EVA process. Take the time to explain to your employees your value discipline and why you have adopted it. Describe your operating model, and give all your employees an opportunity to help refine it through suggestion programs and business improvement teams. The mutual benefits are twofold. These insights and involvement will help reduce the anxiety and helplessness of the "black box" culture, and will increase the level of job satisfaction in that employees can participate in their own job development.

It has been said by some that most hourly workers do not have the financial sophistication to understand the operation of EVA. We find this position both arrogant and demeaning. At the level at which they operate, we have found shop-floor employees who have a native understanding of value creation superior to that of MBA graduates. As the examples previously described have shown, the best and brightest know what levers to pull to reduce cycle time, to reduce inventory, to improve scrap rates, and the like. All they need is familiarity with EVA concepts, which of course requires training, a subject we deal with in the next chapter.

If a successful effort is made to reach the rank and file, it will be easier to persuade the union leadership to adopt EVA as the basis for incentive compensation. From the union point of view, there are two attractive elements to the EVA plan: (1) the cash-adjusting features of the NOPAT and capital calculations eliminate the concern that management might manipulate accruals to reduce the size of the bonus to which workers are entitled and (2) the basic EVA calculation on which bonuses are based is the same within employee groups all the way through senior management. It is fairness incarnate.

A highly persuasive case for shop-floor involvement in EVA was published in 1999 by Stern Stewart Europe, headquartered in London, in a paper entitled "The Capitalist Manifesto: The Transformation of the Corporation—Employee Capitalism," by Erik Stern and Johannes Schonburg. The paper, first of all, describes the enormous boost to participatory management given by European Union governments in recent years. The left-of-center parties in power in Western Europe have long given up on socialism—no one wants to nationalize the "commanding heights of the economy" any more—and are now talking in terms of worker participation in decision making, in return for equity ownership and/or profit sharing. In Germany, of course, there has long been worker (read union) representation on the supervisory boards of corporations, but that has generally been at a far remove from the shop floor. The new initiatives would bring participation down to the workplace, as in the companies we have examined in the United States.

The European Commission published a seminal paper in 1992, "The Promotion of Employee Participation in Profits and Enterprise Results," in which it canvassed the programs in different member states, and presented a recommendation in typical Brussels bureaucratese: "The Council hereby invites the Member States to acknowledge the potential benefits of a wider use of employees in profits and enterprise results either by means of profit sharing, or through employee share ownership or by a combination of both."

In Britain, there has been a remarkable change in the attitude of the Labor government and the attitude and rhetoric of trade unionists, as compared with the combative rhetoric of the past. In

November 1998, Gordon Brown, the Chancellor of the Exchequer, stated, in a Pre-Budget Report to the House of Commons: "As our productivity discussions with business have also revealed, Britain can do more to remove the barriers to opportunity and ambition. . . . I want, through targeted tax reform, to reward long-term commitment by employees and I want to remove, once and for all, the old 'them and us' culture in British industry. I want to encourage the new enterprise culture of teamwork in which everyone contributes and everyone benefits from success. So, in the budget we will make it easier for all employees—and not just a few—to become stakeholders in their company."

In May 1999, the Trades Union Congress (TUC) held a one-day conference in London on partnership with industry, attended by union and management representatives. Prime Minister Tony Blair addressed the assemblage and issued a challenge to the unions: "What is your role? Why do they need you? If you can demonstrate competencies and efficiencies on issues like training, pensions, and safety, then you can find a role in workplace partnership. If you can't, don't be surprised if you're not invited to the party."

The TUC presented a report to the conference called "Partners for Progress: New Unionism in the Workplace," in which it candidly conceded how far the unions had declined in public esteem. It argued that "trade unions should be seen as part of the solution to the UK's problems rather than as a problem themselves. . . . The rhetoric of struggle, strikes, and strife . . . has little resonance in today's world of work. Of course, it is an essential part of the trade union role to continue to expose the bad employer—the bullying boss, the boss who discriminates, or the boss who fails to observe fundamental legal rights. But most workers do not believe that their employer is a bad employer. They may think that their employers could be better managers and they certainly want a greater say in how decisions are made. But put most simply, people want to be proud of and in many cases are proud of the organizations that employ them. . . . Alienated workers will not deliver the high performance that employers now seek."

The report included brief case studies of partnership initiatives in several diverse organizations—the Cooperative Bank, Inland Revenue, Tesco (a large retail chain), British Gas, and Unisys, among others. Partnership involved engaging the workers' representatives in decisions involving corporate strategy, training the workforce, and the dissemination of best practices in the production process. The unions were made privy to confidential information that they never would have seen before. At National Power, for example, the partnership agreement set up a National Business Review Committee "which brings together senior managers [of] the company with full-time officers and lay representatives from the unions." Meeting every half year, the committee is extensively briefed on the company's plans and strategic options, affording "genuine consultation on a basis that is both early enough to influence outcomes and sufficiently well-informed to be really meaningful."

The Stern Stewart paper gleaned from the Web site of the European Trade Union Congress several examples of financial incentives recently offered employees on the continent: "Audi Ag introduced profit sharing for all employees from 1998, with a fixed component based on seniority and a separate variable one. The privatization of Telecom Eireeann (Ireland) will lead to employee share ownership of 15 percent spread among 11,000 workers, while the privatization of Eurocopter and Usinor, the French steel company, provided a similar opportunity. In addition, company-based agreements exist at BP Amoco, Shell, Mobil, Degussa, and Rosenthal. Finally, the chemical sector in Germany has agreed to wealth creation and stock ownership programs. Many other cases exist."

Profit-sharing and stock ownership plans for shop-floor workers are a great step forward as compared to no monetary incentives at all, but the Stern Stewart paper argues that both arrangements have their drawbacks. For one thing, there is no sharing if profits are nonexistent—in contrast to EVA bonus plans that reward participants for an improvement in EVA even if EVA is negative (although this usually means that profits exist). Moreover, profit-sharing plans are dependent on corporate results, and the corporations are usually large, so there is no link with what the individual employee is contributing in his or her division. An EVA plan, by contrast, is typically based on local as well as corporate results.

The distribution of shares and share options has the obvious advantage of giving employees a personal stake in the fortunes of the company, but it has a disadvantage as an incentive in that share prices are often dependent on external forces—the general state of the economy, interest rates, inflation, and/or the state of the industry concerned—not merely on the success of the firm. And, as with profit sharing, there is no linkage with local performance. Beyond these considerations, profit sharing and share distribution are one-way streets—there is gain if the business is profitable and if shares rise in price, but no downside risk. In a typical EVA incentive plan, at least on the executive level, the provision of a bonus bank ensures that participants can lose some of their past winnings if performance declines sufficiently.

In the United States, no shop-floor plan that we know of puts employees' EVA bonus at risk, but Stern and Schonburg describe a remarkable plan in Germany that promises both high rewards and concomitant risks. It was instituted in a company called Sirona Dental Systems, a manufacturer of high-tech dental equipment that Siemens sold to private investors in 1997. The following year, with the help of Stern Stewart, the company installed a fully articulated EVA plan for all 1,200 employees, from the chief executive down to the maintenance staff.

The bulk of the workforce was unionized, with 90 percent covered by a collective bargaining agreement. For this group, the EVA plan was to be voluntary and to have a large element of risk. In

November of each year (1998 being the first), each worker was asked to decide how much of one month's salary—between 40 percent and 80 percent—would be at risk in the following year. The company would then match 50 percent of the employee's designated amount; the combined sum would be the worker's target bonus. Thus, if the employee put up 80 percent of one month's pay, the employer's contribution would bring the target bonus to 120 percent. Say a worker earned a monthly wage of DM5,000; that would mean a target bonus of DM6,000. The EVA performance measured would be that of the worker's operating unit (the same system as in the executive plan). There was also a bonus bank for the workers. If results overshot the target, two-thirds of the excess would go into the bank and one-third would be paid out in cash. In each successive year, one-third of the bank's balance would be distributed, as long as there was a positive balance; all this is typical of an executive plan.

To repeat: the unionized workforce did not have to participate; everything was voluntary. If a worker decided to join the plan, he or she could later change that decision and pull out, but was then not allowed to reenter the plan. The reason: to prevent participants from going in and out, depending on their impression of how well the company was likely to do. There were extensive training sessions for all employees, and when the unionized workforce finally came to decision time in November 1998, 87 percent opted to participate—a remarkable figure, given the risks involved. Fully 81 percent decided to invest the maximum—80 percent of one month's pay.

After the plan got underway, several initiatives were undertaken to improve EVA performance; one was an ambitious companywide plan to reduce inventories. By the end of the first year, Sirona showed an increase in EVA of 125 percent, with a range of 104 percent to 191 percent for individual EVA centers within the company.

No single plan, of course, provides a template appropriate for all situations. Every EVA plan is custom-built to fit the specific business. But there have been enough EVA programs on the shop floor to establish their credibility. The Sirona experience, like that of Briggs & Stratton, has shown that a union will accept an EVA program. Progressive unions in the United States have, on occasion, agreed to profit sharing—for example, the United Auto Workers. If a union will accept profit sharing, it's not such a long step to embrace EVA. In Europe, of course, unions are far stronger, and their cooperation will be more decisive if EVA is to expand on the shop floor. The partnership initiatives in Great Britain and on the Continent, explored in the Stern–Schonburg paper, suggest that the moment has come for an aggressive sales pitch to the unions.

As the paper suggests in its conclusion: "Including employees in the value-creating process will change their entire view of themselves, their colleagues, their superiors, and their company; they will think and act like owners. . . . EVA encourages them to enlarge the pie, from which they earn their share."

Chapter 7

Getting the Message Out:
Training and Communications

There is no more important aspect of installing an EVA program than training the troops. EVA represents a decisive change not only in the way a company measures its performance and rewards its staff but in how it conducts every aspect of its business. With the focus on improving EVA as the new bottom line, all manner of traditional practices will be altered, from incentive systems to the allocation of capital to production processes on the shop floor. Change—often drastic change—is the name of the game, and it is rarely popular.

Change can be rejuvenating to an organization, but to those in the trenches, who are not the promoters of change but are often its objects, the new and unfamiliar are likely to be perceived as threatening. Fear prompts resistance. Resistance can, of course, be overcome by diktat, but the authoritarian management style is hardly to be recommended if the goal is cooperation in effecting change. Far better are explanation and persuasion. If employees are given a clear, detailed description of expected changes and the reasons they are being made, a good deal of anxiety can be blown away.

It is helpful to give employees the experience of viewing the company from the "outside" in a way unfamiliar to most of them. They should be persuaded that the changes are driven by the competitive environment, or by the poor performance of the company's shares, and that if these changes are not made, the long-term survival of the organization is at stake. All this should be part of a formal training program, required by a subject of EVA's complexity.

We present here two approaches to training. The first is that of Briggs & Stratton, which, as described in Chapter 3, adopted EVA as part of a strategic overhaul of the entire company. The second is that of Herman Miller, which embraced the EVA discipline in 1996 without any effort to alter its strategy or products, beyond the normal annual changes in its market offerings. EVA produced many changes, but, at Herman Miller, there was no strategic refocusing similar to Briggs & Stratton's. In that regard, Herman Miller's experience paralleled that of many EVA companies.

At Briggs & Stratton, training for the salaried staff and shop-floor workers in the Milwaukee area began in 1994 and went on for three years; 3,000 individuals passed through the classes, which were conducted by Judy Whipple, the manager of corporate training. Employees had already been exposed to information about EVA in a detailed question-and-answer article in the company newsletter (see Figure 7.1 on pages 110–111), and salaried staff had heard brief discussions in their quarterly meetings, but this exposure was hardly deemed sufficient. In groups of 16 to 20, salaried workers received four hours of training in Whipple's "Managing for Value Creation Workshops," and production line workers got two hours. The sessions were popular. They not only appeased curiosity but meant time off from the job.

Whipple started each session by giving a five-minute written test on what each participant knew about EVA. (She repeated the test at the end, to determine how successful her instruction had been, as she put it.) She then segued into an account of the Briggs

& Stratton strategic restructuring that began after the company's first unprofitable year in decades, in 1989. With flip-chart diagrams and slide projections, she highlighted the reversion of the company to its former strategy of low-cost, high-volume production of multi-purpose engines, and the abandonment of its unprofitable division that had manufactured more high-cost, low-volume engines with more sophisticated features. The company would only continue in the latter business in a joint venture with a partner better equipped to do the low-volume manufacturing.

Following that presentation, Whipple gave a detailed explanation of the Briggs & Stratton "Road Map to Value Creation" (described in Chapter 4) and of how the various boxes in the road map were mutually reinforcing. Then came a discussion of the rationale for EVA, a description of its components, an illustration of how NOPAT is calculated (using a hypothetical example of a company with monthly sales of $100,000), how the capital charge is applied, and how EVA is finally derived. In keeping with the elementary nature of the presentation, Whipple made no effort to discuss the adjustments to the accounting numbers in the progression to NOPAT. The accountants handled that, she explained briskly. Nor did she attempt to explain how the cost of capital was calculated. That was in the hands of Bob Eldridge (then CFO), she said.

There followed a lengthy discussion with the class about how EVA could be increased. Soliciting examples from the group, which was reasonably forthcoming, Whipple stressed three fundamental ways of enlarging EVA: (1) "build" (commit new capital to initiatives that promise a return in excess of the cost of capital); (2) "operate" (increase the cash rate of return without tying up any new capital); and (3) "harvest" (withdraw capital from activities that are not expected to provide an adequate return). To drive home the strategies, Whipple provided some mundane personal examples—the "build" strategy of insulating a home to reduce heating bills, the "harvest" strategy of getting rid of a lemon car.

Managing for Value Creation at Briggs & Stratton

key element in Briggs & Stratton's success over the last few years can be attributed to the unlocking of value through a combination of EVA performance measurement, a re-focused strategy, organizational refinement, and customized incentives. John Shiely, Briggs & Stratton's newly elected President & Chief Operating Officer, provides insight into a new way of looking at business that reveals if a company is creating value or draining its resources.

Q: You have said that our basic business philosophy is "managing for value creation." What does that mean, and how does it relate to EVA?

A: The ultimate goal of any management effort is to effectively manage a corporation's six major constituencies: shareholders, lenders, employees, customers, suppliers and the community. In managing for value creation, we recognize that the first two constituencies (shareholders and lenders) have a legitimate need for a fair return on the capital they contribute to the business. This is called the "cost of capital." We recognize a further obligation to create value for our shareholders over and above the cost of capital. This imperative can only be met by superior value creation. Real value creation requires an integrative process of managing the four non-capital providing corporate constituencies (employees, customers, suppliers, and community) toward the end of creating value. We have attempted to capture this concept in our "Model of Value Creation." EVA is simply the *unbiased* yardstick for determining whether we are creating value.

Q: What are the primary methods

of value creation and how have we pursued these methods at Briggs & Stratton?

A: The primary methods of value creation are re-focusing of our strategy, re-configuration of our organization structure and systems, and re-engineering of our designs and processes.

So when you hear of such strategies as focusing on high value mass application products, organization structure changes such as divisionalization and focus factories, and re-engineering efforts such as BIT teams and cell manufacturing, you should understand that the goal of all of this is value creation. A more detailed chart of these methods as employed specifically at Briggs & Stratton has been formulated. We must all understand that superior value creation ultimately requires *changes* in the things we do and how we do them.

Q: What major factors influenced management's decision to develop a value creation management program?

A: By 1990 it became clear that we were not managing our capital very efficiently. We were employing three times the amount of capital in operating assets to produce the same level of income as we were in the 1970s. The "old" Briggs & Stratton approaches to achieving our solid competitive position as the industry leader, such as excess capacity, high vertical integration, batch processes, and limited product offerings, which were once competitive benefits, became competitive drawbacks. The economies of combined operations, internal control and coordination which these approaches offered years ago, had given way to dulled incentives, burdensome capital

calls, technological isolationism and a loss of performance focus on the human resource side. In other words, our operations were not "right" for the 1990s.

Today's competition is global and intense, and it became clear that we could not continue to manage our company the same way we did for the last several decades and just pass along price increases to the customer. A market which had become more concentrated in the hands of mass retailers made this painfully clear to us. In such an environment, companies must create value by managing costs, improving operating efficiencies, and deploying capital carefully. Companies that do not do this will not stay competitive and will eventually fail.

Q: What is EVA?

A: EVA is a means of measuring performance, and is simply a company's cash earnings minus the cost of the capital needed to produce those earnings. When a company produces a cash return greater than the cost of its capital, it has created economic value. This is called having a positive EVA. A negative EVA shows that a company is draining its resources.

Q: Explain what you mean by "cost of capital?"

A: Begin with the assumption that capital (machines, computers, inventory, facilities) costs money. The cost of this money is related to the amount of risk our shareholders and lenders are willing to absorb. A "risk free" 30 year US Treasury bond currently yields almost 8 percent interest. A stock of companies of average risk have historically provided a return 6 percent in excess of the

Figure 7.1   Text of Briggs & Stratton employee newsletter

risk free rate. Since Briggs & Stratton is a company with about average risk, our stock has a cost of capital of about 14 percent. As the risk on bonds is much lower, our debt capital has a significantly lower cost of capital. The average of our stock and debt cost of capital for this year is 11.7 percent. This is our cost of capital.

Q: What purpose does the EVA program serve?

A: The purpose of the EVA value management program is to link Briggs & Stratton's performance measurement and incentives to the goals of our capital providers or owners of the company. We recognize that we have a basic obligation to create value for our shareholders and lenders, and we do this by delivering value to our employees, customers, suppliers, and the community.

Q: If someone doesn't have anyone reporting to them, how can they "manage" for value creation?

A: First of all you manage the most important person to the process – yourself. You need to insure that all of your activities are value directed. Secondly, while many employees do not manage a lot of people they do manage some very expensive capital in the form of machines in the plant and computers in the office. Employees can also have an impact on large amounts of capital tied up in inventory by the way they perform their work.

Q: What kinds of things can employees do to create value?

A: There are thousands of big and little things that can be done everyday to create value, which when added up has a tremendous impact on EVA. An engineer might come up with a new muffler design which improves quality, reduces cost by 5 cents and eliminates the need for one of the expensive machines currently needed to produce it.

An office worker might find a creative way to use his or her current computer to perform a new task more efficiently, without having to invest capital in a new computer. An assembler might come up with a better way to configure their assembly process in order to reduce inventory or improve efficiency. Everything we do should be viewed as a small business where improved productivity increases cash returns, and keeping our capital under control minimizes our cost of capital, with the result that the value of the business is increased. You might view EVA as taking a billion dollar company and breaking it down into a Seven/Eleven convenience store. You start with cash in a cigar box. You use the cash to buy goods for the shelves. You sell the goods, pay expenses, including capital costs, and put the remaining cash back in the cigar box. If at the end of the year there is more cash in the cigar box than there was at the beginning of the year, you have created value (i.e. had a positive EVA for the year).

Q: How has this value driven restructuring benefited the company?

A: The benefits from the restructuring have been substantial: bet-

ter product line focus, improved financial accountability, better assessment of labor/capital trade-offs, and internal development of experienced operational general managers.

Q: Summarize the results of value creation at Briggs & Stratton.

A: Managing for value creation has led to an increase in the value of Briggs & Stratton's stock. And that's not surprising because stock value is the market's assessment of how a particular company manages investor's capital. Our stock jumped from about $22 per share in 1992 to more than $80 at the end of 1993. We have proven that we are a good enough investment to attract capital, and capital is the fuel that makes any enterprise go. Also, as many of you may know, a high stock price is the best defense against any type of hostile takeover.

Q: How does that translate into a better future for the company and its employees?

A: A company cannot deliver superior value to its shareholders unless it engages all of its constituencies in an effort to provide high value job opportunities to its employees, high value products to its customers, high value partnerships with its suppliers and high value relationships with the communities in which it does business. The better we get at managing for value creation, the brighter the future for everyone involved.

Figure 7.1   (Continued)

After a coffee break, the class tackled an EVA simulation involving management of a convenience store:

"The Jiffy store is located on a county highway, nicely situated between the town of Cashville and several large subdivisions. You are the owner and have two full-time and two part-time employees.

"Your Jiffy store is open from 6 A.M. to midnight and stocks only the following eight items: white milk, eggs, butter, white bread, wheat bread, cereals, canned goods, and soda pop. You average approximately 100 customers per day with sales of about $500 per day. Early morning and early evening are your busiest hours (roughly between 6:30–9 A.M. and 3:30–8:00 P.M.).

"You currently have three coolers. Your main/largest cooler is in good condition and requires very little upkeep. You use one of the two smaller coolers to store excess milk, eggs, and butter. Your third cooler is used as a backup for unanticipated cooler breakdowns. You did have to use it once last year when the small cooler broke down for a few hours. Employees use the backup cooler for soda, snacks, and lunch items. You keep it running because once it's off, it takes about six hours to get it cold enough to store other items.

"In the main cooler there are eight racks for milk; each holds 36 gallons. Total capacity is 288 gallons. You also store 100 dozen eggs and 200 pounds of butter in the main cooler. Your smaller cooler holds about 90 gallons of milk, 50 dozen eggs, and 350 pounds of butter. The third cooler, which isn't very reliable, has about the same capacity. Both white and wheat bread are displayed on bread racks that can each hold about 250 loaves."

The class was also given figures for the store's monthly sales, costs of goods sold, general and administrative expenses, taxes, adjustments to cash, capital employed, and cost of capital. All were asked to compute the store's NOPAT and EVA. Thereafter, Whipple solicited suggestions as to how the store's EVA could be improved. They came in abundance—adding merchandise lines (cigarettes, among others), getting rid of the third cooler, shortening hours, and, if Cashville was in Nevada, installing slot machines. That got a big laugh.

The session then went on to a discussion of how the EVA approach could improve performance in the participants' own jobs. They were regrouped so that each table had people in the same or similar fields, after which they brainstormed for a time to come up with specific ideas for improvement. Some were quite imaginative, though there were comments that they needed more time and more information on costs and feasibility.

In August 1999, the current refresher training course was introduced on the corporate intranet. It is available to any employee who has access to a PC. The course covers both the Briggs & Stratton Road Map to Value Creation and a guide to EVA—its rationale and methods of calculation. A variety of hypothetical EVA exercises, of varying complexity, are offered; the employee is given basic data and encouraged to make the relevant calculations and come up with the answer. The correct answer is then provided. The refresher course has hardly swept the company, but it had an average of 85 hits a month for its first nine months. It has been an effective supplement to the basic training course.

The advantage of the Briggs & Stratton system is that the training was consistent, what with one leader and an assistant shouldering the whole burden. But it took a long time. At Herman Miller, as at many other companies (SPX, for one), the system was one of training the trainers. Under the direction of Ray Bennett, a veteran training specialist, a team of eight to ten people was put together to train the "facilitators" (Herman Miller eschews the term "foremen"), who in turn instructed the people they supervised. Bennett points out that there is no better way of mastering a subject than having to expound it to someone else. It's almost as good as having to write an essay oneself. Moreover, HM felt a degree of urgency. Training began in October 1996, with a course called EVA 101. It had to be completed by December 1, when the bonus plan for the rank-and-file was to switch to the EVA calculation. In all, some 5,000 people at Herman Miller North America, the principal domestic unit at the time, underwent the training.

EVA 101, the elementary course, was to be followed later by more advanced training. Facilitators were provided with an elaborate guidebook, which outlined the agenda for the classes they were to hold. A brisk pace was outlined for each two-hour session: 5 minutes for "Welcome, Expectations, and Review of Agenda"; 5 minutes for an initial knowledge test; 15 minutes for a discussion of "Why EVA?"; roughly 40 minutes for EVA calculation, terminology, and definitions; 15 minutes for the 60/11 Rule and practice; 8 minutes for a video featuring Joel Stern; 20 minutes for "Our Earned Share" (the bonus plan); 5 minutes for another knowledge test; and 10 minutes for closing questions and review of other learning materials.

The flavor and candor of the presentation can be sampled by these suggested "Answers to a Few Common Questions":

"*What is EVA?* EVA means Economic Value Added. EVA is actually a measurement or calculation of the amount of value or worth of our company. . . . It's Net Operating Profit after Taxes (NOPAT) less a charge for the cost of capital. When applying the EVA concept to our business, we expect to achieve yearly improvement, which means the economic value of Herman Miller is growing.

"*Why are we using EVA?* We're using EVA as a tool to help Herman Miller grow its value to shareholders, customers, and employees. During the past 10 years, from 1985–1995, we did a poor job of creating value. In fact, for every dollar our shareholders invested in the company, we destroyed two dollars of value. That's like putting $1,000 into a savings account and finding out next year it has a market value of $500. How happy with your investment would you be then? Would you put more money into that account, or would you take your money out and put it some place else? If Herman Miller stock does for our shareholders what this savings account did for you . . . our shareholders would take their money away from Herman Miller and invest it elsewhere. This could be very bad for us. In fact, that could severely hurt our company.

"Running our business with a focus on EVA is critical to our future. When EVA improves, our market value should improve. And, if our market value improves, Herman Miller will be a healthier company. A healthier Herman Miller, Inc. means better rewards and a more secure future for employees and shareholders."

The presentation became somewhat more sophisticated when the discussion turned to EVA terminology, the EVA calculation, and the "60/11" rule. The progression of numbers leading to the calculation of NOPAT went into considerable detail, in such matters as the cost of goods sold, operating expenses, and overhead. As at Briggs & Stratton, there was no treatment of the adjustments to accounting figures to reflect economic value, except in the case of capitalizing operating leases. Nor was there any discussion about how the cost of capital was determined.

Considerable detail was offered, however, as to what constitutes capital, in order to prepare the way for a discussion about conserving it. The distinction was made between investment capital and working capital, with definitions of inventory and accounts receivable: "How is this an investment we make? Answer: We are 'floating' the money for the product until the customer pays us; sometimes it takes several months, if they don't have a complete installation. For EVA we need to make it easier for customers to pay us." As for accounts payable, it's "like the opposite of accounts receivable. It's the money we owe our suppliers, so it's equal to negative capital (we're using their cash, much the same way you use your credit card and hold off paying for 30 days)." The facilitator's guide discreetly failed to suggest that payments be delayed as long as possible.

All this is preliminary to a discussion of improving EVA through application of the "60/11" rule: if expenses are reduced by $1.00, EVA will increase by 60 cents (figuring the company's tax rate at 40 percent). If $1.00 of capital is saved, the saving will be 11 cents annually (the cost of capital is calculated to be 11 percent). All this assumes, of course, that everything else remains the same— that there are no offsetting increases in expenses to change that $1.00 reduction in costs, and no increase in capital employed. The facilitator then leads the class through an example or two. The session ends with a discussion of how an improvement in EVA affects the bonus plan.

EVA 201, which began at Herman Miller North America in February 1997, concentrated on the impact on EVA of changes in production practices, inventory, and investment; the goal was to demonstrate the link between what employees did on the job and the final result. The instructor led the class through a typical "EVA impact situation" and then asked the class members to analyze other situations to determine whether EVA would increase or decrease.

One example: "To produce a new product, we had to buy a $1 million machine and hire 25 additional direct and indirect production workers. After covering cost of goods sold, operating expenses, and taxes, we determined NOPAT is $5 million higher than it would have been without the product. "Was investing in this product the right thing to do? Answer: The sales increase drove a positive NOPAT and would have more than covered the added capital charge of the machine and probably some increase in accounts receivable." So EVA was up.

Another: "Fifty work-surface blanks have been cut to the wrong dimension. They will become scrap. Answer: Overhead costs are up because we had to scrap 50 work surfaces. Direct labor costs may be increased, depending on production schedules or if overtime is needed to run the replacement work surfaces. Capital remains the same because the original work surfaces were expensed to overhead and the replacement work surfaces were considered inventory." So EVA declines.

These exercises were followed by a "not so good" scenario—an example of the hit EVA can take when a production error occurs. In the hypothetical example, Herman Miller, Inc., had an order for 100 chairs, which, if everything had gone well, would have produced a net sale figure of $50,000, from which were to be deducted $34,500 in cost of goods sold and $9,000 in operating expenses, for a $6,500 net operating profit before tax and a NOPAT of $3,900 after taxes of $2,600. After deduction of a capital charge of $2,255, the bottom line would have been a positive EVA of $1,645.

But everything did not go well. The wrong fabric was sewn onto the chairs, which made them unacceptable to the customer. Instead of the order fetching $50,000, the chairs had to be discounted at a Herman Miller store and sold for a mere $28,124, minus $1,000 for the cost of return freight. With the same cost of goods sold and operating expenses and an increase of $500 in the capital charge (because of an increase in accounts receivable and inventory for an additional three weeks), the result was a negative EVA of $12,581. However vicarious, it was a chastening lesson.

All this was by way of introduction to what, at Herman Miller, is called the EVA Driver Tree—the progression from net sales to EVA. In the exercises that followed, the class was given the data of sales, cost of sales, operating expenses, and so on, of a hypothetical company and asked to compute its EVA. Then it was asked to compute the effect on EVA of a growth in sales of 30 percent, using the same percentage relationships of expenses to sales as in the first example. That done, the assignment was to calculate the impact on EVA of a productivity improvement that decreased the cost of goods sold by 2 percent. The improvement in EVA was much larger.

The class was now introduced to Herman Miller's EVA Driver Tree for the second quarter of fiscal 1997—a vast array of linked boxes that break down every component of the linear progression from net sales to NOPAT to EVA. For most items in that vertical declination, there are horizontal lines to boxes that represent the relevant components. Thus, net sales consist of intercompany sales and net trade sales, with the latter leading to nine other components, including trade discounts and freight costs. The cost of sales has, as its components, materials, direct labor, and overhead. The point of the array is to show how changes in the various branches of the tree affect the trunk line from net sales to EVA.

The classroom session ended, as did the one described at Briggs & Stratton, with members of the class asked to brainstorm ideas for EVA improvements in their work areas. Participants were told "to select their highest potential EVA improvement idea and go back to the driver tree to circle the specific cells that might not be obvious. For example: Increasing direct shipments will not only reduce inventory but will lead to fewer needs for buildings, warehouse space, and land." The class was also reminded of the utility of the 60/11 rule. If anyone, for example, came up with a proposal to use a less expensive adhesive that resulted in savings of just $1,000 a year, that bright character would have "personally increased EVA by $600." Behind the exhortations was the belief that workers at bench or keyboard constitute a vast resource of knowledge and imagination that managers would be foolhardy to ignore.

As important as formal training, at the onset of an EVA program, is continuous communication with the workforce. Monthly EVA reports by business units are commonplace at EVA companies, but the information is often closely held. At Briggs & Stratton, there are monthly meetings for 15 to 20 top staff people in each of the five operating divisions. They discuss the EVA data, which they then filter out to much of the flock. Quarterly meetings are held for salaried staff at corporate headquarters, where an elaborate slide show presents the EVA numbers in great detail. Videotapes of the meeting are then sent to Briggs & Stratton installations around the country.

The quarterly meeting on August 5, 1999, was typical of the detail presented, but was perhaps jollier than usual because fiscal 1999, which ended June 30, was a banner year. Sales were up 13 percent to $1.5 billion over the prior year, and net income was up 50 percent to $106 million. EVA rose to $39.7 million, compared to a target of $20.7 million and a projection of $33.4 million. The EVA performance factor for the company as a whole came to 1.70, which meant a 70 percent excess bonus for the corporate component—50 percent of the total bonus for salaried staff in the divisions, the other 50 percent being dependent on divisional results. Three of the divisions—Spectrum, castings, and die cast—had performance factors greater than 2. Although some small units had negative EVA, it was the company's best EVA performance ever, largely accounted for by higher unit volume and surprisingly low aluminum prices. (Aluminum engine blocks are a big item at Briggs.) Employees were to get their annual bonus checks on August 17. Anybody with a pencil could calculate what the bonus would be. And prospects were bright for an even better performance the following year.

At Herman Miller, regular communication with the workforce is even more frequent. Every month, the company issues a commercially produced video, generally 15 to 30 minutes long, called Business Exchange. For an extended period, it was presided over by David Guy, vice president for finance at Herman Miller North America until he was promoted in April 1999 to be a senior vice president at Herman Miller, Inc. and general manager of Zeeland operations. In an interview format with another Miller executive, such as then CFO Brian Walker (he is now president of Herman Miller North America), Guy would offer the EVA Driver Tree for the month—the full report from net sales to the month's EVA, with a discussion of why results were good or poor.

The rest of the video would be devoted to other corporate news, a visit to a trade show where Herman Miller carried off a prize, even a segment about how employees were contributing to the relief effort for Kosovo. The video for July 1999 produced the cheerful news that the quarterly bonus would be 9.1 percent, a surprise after forecasts of no bonus at all. The reason: sales were unexpectedly good in June, the international division had done very well and the company had been more successful than expected in its drive for cost control. And not to be overlooked was a trick of the calendar—there was one more week in June of 1999 than in 1998. The video concluded with a playful account, snappily edited, about how unfounded rumors can spread

Herman Miller—Continental North America

EVA Driver Tree - Results (in 000's)

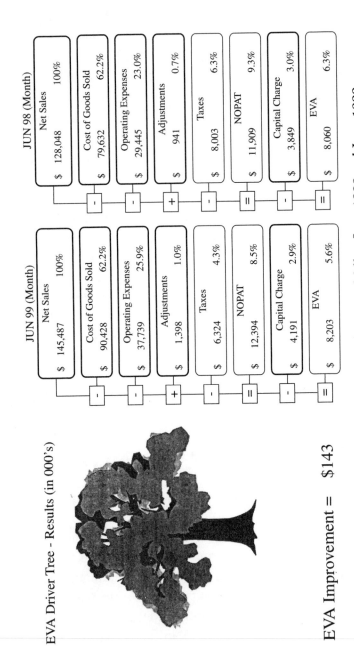

JUN 99 (Month)		
Net Sales	100%	
$	145,487	
Cost of Goods Sold	62.2%	
$	90,428	
Operating Expenses	25.9%	
$	37,739	
Adjustments	1.0%	
$	1,398	
Taxes	4.3%	
$	6,324	
NOPAT	8.5%	
$	12,394	
Capital Charge	2.9%	
$	4,191	
EVA	5.6%	
$	8,203	

JUN 98 (Month)		
Net Sales	100%	
$	128,048	
Cost of Goods Sold	62.2%	
$	79,632	
Operating Expenses	23.0%	
$	29,445	
Adjustments	0.7%	
$	941	
Taxes	6.3%	
$	8,003	
NOPAT	9.3%	
$	11,909	
Capital Charge	3.0%	
$	3,849	
EVA	6.3%	
$	8,060	

EVA Improvement = $143

Figure 7.2   EVA Driver Tree Page: EVA Improvement; Herman Miller, June 1998 and June 1999

120

Herman Miller—Continental North America

EVA Driver Tree - Results (in 000's)

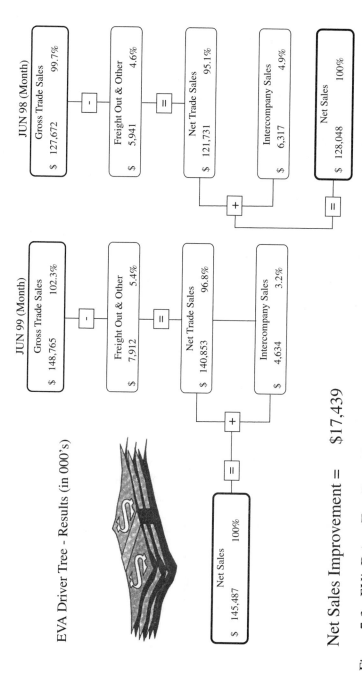

JUN 99 (Month)

Gross Trade Sales   102.3%
$ 148,765

−

Freight Out & Other   5.4%
$ 7,912

=

Net Trade Sales   96.8%
$ 140,853

Intercompany Sales   3.2%
$ 4,634

+

=

Net Sales   100%
$ 145,487

JUN 98 (Month)

Gross Trade Sales   99.7%
$ 127,672

−

Freight Out & Other   4.6%
$ 5,941

=

Net Trade Sales   95.1%
$ 121,731

Intercompany Sales   4.9%
$ 6,317

+

Net Sales   100%
$ 128,048

=

Net Sales Improvement = $17,439

Figure 7.3 EVA Driver Tree Page: Net Sales Improvement; Herman Miller, June 1998 and June 1999

121

in an organization. Employees were urged to tap reliable sources of information, like the company's intranet.

The video is distributed to every department in the company in the United States, and workers spend an hour or so in a conference room with their supervisors, viewing the screen and discussing the substance. Even more information is available every month on the intranet. It can be viewed on a PC or at an "electronic kiosk," a stand-up PC on the shop floor, shown in the July 1999 video. The full monthly Driver Tree, totaling 10 pages if printed out, is available. (The first two pages for June 1999 are reproduced in Figures 7.2 and 7.3).

The Driver Tree is presented vertically in this format. The first page for June 1999, for example, has two columns, comparing the month with June 1998: net sales, cost of goods sold, operating expenses, adjustments, taxes, NOPAT, capital charge, and EVA. If you click on net sales, you bring up another page giving its components for the two months. Click on cost of goods sold and you have, on page 3, the numbers for materials, direct labor, and overhead, plus figures for gross margins and the volume of bonus dollars in the overhead figures for the two months. Even more detail is offered if you call up operating expenses, which includes the company's R&D expenditures for the month.

Isn't Herman Miller worried that some of these data might leak, to its competitive disadvantage? Not at all, we were told; the company is more concerned about having an uninformed workforce. There seems little danger of that.

Chapter 8

EVA and Acquisitions

Much of the history of American capitalism is the history of mergers and acquisitions. Typically, a new industry would emerge with a multiplicity of players. Later, a winnowing out would occur, a process of consolidation effected through business failure and, inexorably, by the absorption of the weaker brethren by more aggressive and better financed competitors. Starting in the nineteenth century, that was the history of the railroads, the oil industry, telephones, steel, and, in the twentieth century, autos, the airlines, and aircraft manufacture. At the end of the twentieth century, the same process was at work in the various branches of the computer industry and telecommunications, though those arenas are so dynamic that consolidation in some segments is accompanied by the proliferation of new entrants in others.

In the era of the "robber barons," the famous 1930ish phrase of Matthew Josephson that has become part of the folk memory, the goal of consolidation was often the creation of monopoly power. To the extent that the goal was achievable, the benefits accruing to shareholder value—a term not yet in currency—were so obvious as not to require precise calibration.

In the modern era, of course, monopoly power has been beyond the aspiration of most companies, however large; even oligopolistic power is harder to maintain, what with global competition, as in the auto industry, and rapid technological change, as in steel, telecommunications, and computers. The motive for acquisition must perforce be the creation of additional value on the part of the acquiring company—reflected, of course, in a rise in its share price. (Additional value also has to accrue to the seller's shareholders, by way of a premium, unless the seller is on the ropes.) To be sure, added value is not always achieved, and often it is only the stated motive, the rationale, of the acquiring company, whose leaders may be animated by little more than personal aggrandizement. To preside over a bigger entity means bigger salaries, greater perks, and enhanced prestige.

EVA analysis, as we shall see, is an excellent method of calculating the impact of a proposed acquisition—whether it creates value, and if so, how much. But it does not provide the nonfinancial criteria for evaluating the wisdom of an acquisition; it is no guide to a shopping list of target companies. For that we are dependent on a variety of strategic considerations.

One strategy that clearly failed for most companies was represented by the conglomerate movement that was popular from the 1950s to the mid-1970s. Since the early 1980s, divestiture (unbundling, the Europeans call it) has rid us of most conglomerates. So horrid has this form of organization become in the eyes of investors that chief executives take great pains to avoid having their firms tagged with the name. This despite the fact that some of the most successful companies are indeed conglomerates, and their chief executives are highly regarded—people such as General Electric's Jack Welch, Berkshire Hathaway's Warren Buffett, and Allied Signal's Larry Bossidy, all of whom have created huge shareholder value during the past 20 years. A list of successful conglomerates might also include Minnesota Mining & Manufacturing, Litton Industries, and Tyco.

The continued prosperity of the exceptions raises questions about what created the conglomerate wave and why so many have been dismantled since 1980. The period from the 1950s to the 1970s produced euphoric pronouncements about conglomerates, and investors flocked to them with expectations of synergy gains, cost savings in managing diverse businesses, management expertise in cross-marketing, and reduced capital costs due to corporate diversification. The cyclical movements of diverse businesses were expected to offset each other, thereby smoothing out earnings and cash flow, which would inexorably rise if the businesses were successful. And the early conglomerates did perform. Those that stood out included Litton Industries and groups started by Litton alumni, such as Teledyne and Walter Kidde.

So where did the conglomerates go wrong? The main problem in the 1960s came from the great influx of newcomers, hell-bent to turn themselves into corporate goliaths, who bid up acquisition prices to unrealistic levels. The result was a collapse of the return on assets, once the price paid for takeovers was placed on the buyer's balance sheet. Many buyers tried to disguise the premium by "pooling" accounting, in which the premium paid for the acquisition disappears as if the merged company had always been one. This sleight of hand obscures the fact that acquisitions are investments, and the acquirer's shareholders lay out the capital. In the early 1970s, investors began to get wise to the accounting puzzle and, by the mid-1970s, price–earnings ratios had plummeted to 3 or 4, down from 20 to 25 in 1969. Investors increasingly realized that they could get diversification more cheaply by buying shares for their own portfolios at the going market price.

Thus, the problem with most conglomerates, basically, was that they did not produce synergies or create financial or operating

efficiencies that more than offset the high costs of putting them together. What gains were expected were fully paid for—or more than
fully paid for—in advance, with companies competing against each
other to win the trophy. To repeat, there have been exceptions. And
those are generally the conglomerates that have paid reasonable premiums for acquired businesses and achieved real integrating efficiencies (i.e., synergies post-acquisition). So the lesson seems to
have been well learned; almost everybody eschews diversification
and seeks synergy. Synergy, however, has often been elusive, and
more than a few CEOs have been sacrificed in its vain pursuit. The
reason is undoubtedly that projecting the economic impact of integrating efficiencies and other initiatives to improve operating performance in a merger is more art than science. H. Kurt Christensen,
of the J.L. Kellogg School of Management, at Northwestern University, in an unpublished paper, "Note on the Concept of Synergy," has
identified three common errors made in assessing synergy:

"1. Much more attention is typically paid to assessing potential positive synergy, while far less is paid to potential negative synergy. . . .
2. Unrealistic expectations of operating improvements after purchase are often created, partly because of the failure to decompose
experience into its important subcategories. 3. The process is treated
too much as only a rational analytic process, with too little consideration given to the implementation feasibility of the combination."

With regard to the third item, Andrew Parsons, in his article,
"The Hidden Value Key to Successful Acquisition" (*Business Horizons*, March/April 1984), presents the so-called scientific model of
the acquisition process, the traditional company-driven approach.

Particularly popular in the 1970s and 1980s, and still in use by
many companies today, the scientific approach starts with setting
criteria for the acquisition. These criteria are often more related
to the corporate development executive's "wish list," based on

manageability and risk profile, than on any concrete analysis of the value opportunity. A particular set of criteria might read as follows: (1) $100 million to $500 million in revenue. (2) At least 15 percent compounded annual earnings growth rate for the last five years. (3) Consumer durable goods company. (4) Nonunion facilities. (5) Assembly-type operations ("screwdriver factories"), assembling components manufactured elsewhere. (6) Industry leadership position, defined as at least 30 percent market share. (7) Return on equity in excess of 20 percent.

These parameters are then fed into a Compustat or Mergex type of database, and the resulting output is then screened in terms of industry attractiveness (perhaps using the Michael Porter analysis). The potential target companies are themselves screened to eliminate clear outliers. Finally, a due diligence review is performed on the remaining targets, the final target is chosen, and a deal is struck. When the acquisition is completed, the acquiring company uses the next several months to learn the acquired company's business and then applies its superior management skills to make it a big winner.

It's hard to criticize a process that is supported by so much discipline and quantitative analysis—right? Wrong. This approach can result in identifying, as attractive candidates, many firms in totally unrelated industries with very limited prospects for integrating efficiencies with the company that acquires them. As Parsons notes, "something had been missing in all that scientific screening." We would say that *something* involves detailed knowledge of the competencies and resources of the potential target firms, especially in relation to the operational capabilities of the acquiring company itself.

Parsons rightly contends that the surest way to improve an acquisition program's chances for success is to focus first on an analysis of one's own corporate skills, competitive strengths, and strategic aspirations, and then to use the resulting insights to shape a set of criteria to define the universe of candidates for financial screening.

A company that has embraced our concept of managing for value creation already has a leg up here. In the process of developing a Road Map for Value Creation, as described in Chapter 4, it has not only defined its exploitable skills but has also identified the supporting winning strategies, organizational structures, and key design and process requirements. It will then select target businesses that can help it extend its road map. Only at that point should financial screening and due diligence take place. When the target company is finally taken over, the acquiring company will not be faced with a learning process, but will have a strategy in hand for the unit.

In any event, it should be kept in mind that good deal-making skills are also required for a successful acquisition program. It does little good to identify a superb strategic target if you fail to identify the lurking, potentially fatal, off-balance-sheet hazards—whether they involve litigation, environmental problems, questions of quality or technology, or hidden liabilities derived from contracts with recourse—that would be discovered with a superior due-diligence effort. Keen negotiating skills are also required to avoid paying an excessive acquisition premium, a bargaining process in which EVA calculations are of signal importance.

So we have a well-defined goal and an integrative model for our acquisition process. How do we analyze our prospects for tackling this greased pig of synergy? The answer is that there are two parameters that have the greatest effect on the likelihood of success: the types of products or services produced by the acquired business and the nature of the potential integrating efficiencies. The interaction of these two parameters is represented by Figure 8.1.

Note that the acquisitions with the greatest potential are those that involve products in the acquirer's existing product base, which have obvious prospects for operational synergies. But this is a continuum, and there are, nonetheless, real opportunities to create value farther down in the synergy food chain.

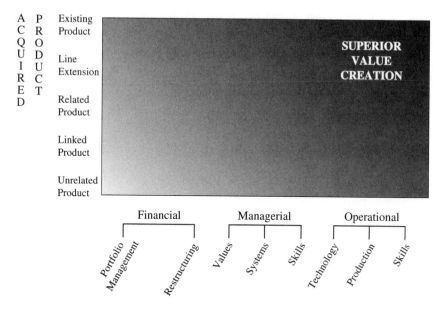

Figure 8.1   Analysis of Prospects for Achieving EVA-Driving Integrating Efficiencies

Turning first to the horizontal axis, we have identified financial synergies as having the most limited prospects for value creation (Christensen, op. cit.). Portfolio management involves attempting to identify undervalued or capital-starved companies, and then providing or withholding capital from the resulting portfolio of companies, depending on their classification in terms of growth and profit profiles (i.e., "dogs," "cash cows," "stars," and "problem children"). Even if you have a skeptical view of the efficiency of markets, you would undoubtedly accept the view that pure capital synergies are limited. If you believe that your only growth opportunities are through portfolio management, it might be a better idea to reorganize as a company like Berkshire Hathaway or give the excess capital back to your shareholders.

The restructurer goes one step further and actually contributes some hands-on effort in pruning underperforming or nonstrategic units and improving the organizational structure and focus of what's left. Because there is a market for "cut and gut" talent that is nearly as efficient as that for companies themselves, this is a source for integrating efficiencies that is only slightly more promising than portfolio management.

The opportunities to mine value in an acquisition become considerably more concrete as we move into the subcategories of managerial synergies. The ability to install a strong quality regimen or customer focus in the acquired company can contribute to an appreciable increase in economic value, as can the introduction of more effective business systems, such as information systems, pay systems, and the like. In the right case, the transfer of superior skills in such areas as inbound and outbound logistics, marketing, and operations architecture can deliver better-than-average results in creating economic value. Not to speak, of course, of the advantages of an EVA-based management system, with its great emphasis on the cost of capital in every aspect of the business.

By far the most fertile ground for value creation in acquisitions is in the area of operational synergies, because they have the potential not only for substantially reducing costs but also for driving revenue growth through broader exploitation of the fixed cost and capital bases of the merged companies. If the technology advances of one company are effectively exploited by the other, value is created, as is also obviously the case if production facilities can be consolidated, resulting in economies of scale. Integration of efficiencies in the distribution area may result from the more extensive distribution channels of the merged company, broader exploitation of the brand identities of both businesses, or the broadening of the service network.

Turning to the vertical axis, we note that the greatest potential for integrating efficiencies is in the acquisition of companies that have product lines comparable to those of the acquirer. The acquirer is likely to understand clearly the competitive and operational challenges of the business and will be able, rather quickly, to realize economies of scale, distribution, and product development. Another result of such an acquisition may be the ability to raise prices, which is of course why some acquisitions of competitive companies are foreclosed by antitrust considerations.

Acquisitions of companies offering products that would provide line extensions for the acquirer represent the next level of potential value creation. These kinds of acquisitions allow the acquirer to increase its core business without venturing too far from home. At most, the acquirer would have to make modest adjustments to its strategic road map.

At the next level is the acquisition of a related product. An example might be the acquisition of an irrigation system for golf courses by a company making, say, mowers for fairways and greens. The acquirer would hope to leverage its understanding of the turf-care business and its established relationships with greens keepers to create value.

Linked products are those that exist in totally unrelated businesses but are somehow linked in terms of technology, production process, or distribution. An example might be the acquisition, by a producer of commercial avionics equipment, of a company making global positioning units for autos—the electronic equipment on the dashboard that gives the position of the car on a city grid and advises the driver on how best to proceed to his destination. The potential for synergy is in the exploitation of similar technology. This is obviously a more tenuous opportunity for value creation, and it requires an extraordinary organization to accomplish the transfer. Finally, we note that the prospects of achieving synergies through the acquisition of unrelated products are extremely limited.

We might review a few notable acquisitions to demonstrate the application of this analysis. Some years ago, Sears acquired Dean Witter with the expectation that its strong retail distribution network (operational synergy) would contribute to the growth of Dean

Witter's retail brokerage business (unrelated business). The economic disappointment is predicted in our model. On the other hand, Sears' foray into the credit-card business with the Discover card (related product) was a successful exploitation of distribution (operational) synergies. While not technically an acquisition, the venture illustrated the benefit of the two-jump move up the synergy model to a related product.

An excellent example of optimal synergy (existing product/operational integrating efficiencies) is provided by Fiserv, Inc., which furnishes banks and other financial institutions with data-processing services. Fiserv has aggressively acquired smaller firms engaged in the same business and has effectively exploited economies of scale and distribution to the great benefit of its shareholders.

We should caution again that synergy analysis is only one piece of the puzzle. Realized synergies may still not compensate for an excessive acquisition premium or a flawed analysis of the target's competitive and operational challenges, or its projected growth profile. The experience of Quaker Oats a few years back is instructive here. By any measure, Quaker's acquisition of Gatorade (a related product) and its exploitation of its retail distribution (operational) synergies to promote Gatorade was a major value creator. The same formula was applied to Snapple, but the EVA bottom line was disastrous. Although it appears that Quaker's distribution capability was somewhat less helpful for a premium beverage like Snapple than it had been for Gatorade, the value game was probably less lost in unrealized synergies than it was in the acquisition premium and the unrealistic projections for Snapple's growth.

How can an excessive premium be avoided? We turn now to an account of the considerations that guided the SPX Corporation in its 1998 purchase of the General Signal Corporation. SPX, based in Muskegon, Michigan, was a long-established producer of parts for auto manufacturers as well as specialized tools and diagnostic equipment sold both to franchised auto dealers and independent repair shops.

General Signal, by contrast, consisted of 15 separate businesses, only one of which had anything to do with autos. The others were in such fields as electrical controls, pumps of various kinds, power systems, radio frequency transmission systems, and much else. So all but one of General Signal's businesses were totally unrelated to SPX's products, which placed the merger at the bottom of the vertical axis in Figure 8.1. The merger, however, was midway on the horizontal axis, for it was premised on significant financial and managerial efficiencies—basically because of EVA, as well as the elimination of General Signal's headquarters staff and other redundant activities. The combined company would initially have $2.5 billion in sales, with a little more than half coming from General Signal's business lines.

SPX CEO John B. Blystone, who was to retain that position in the merged company, announced that "SPX's leadership team intends to apply our proven EVA-based management techniques to create value in General Signal's businesses, as we've done at SPX." That was a key point in the grand design. Thus, although there were no significant synergies in the merger, the same EVA measurement, incentive, and management systems that had caused a dramatic turnaround at SPX since Blystone took over that dispirited company in 1995, would now be relentlessly applied in the new organization. So would "stretch"—another ingredient for which Blystone has become famous. "Stretch" involves ambitious targets, seemingly impossible to achieve because they are beyond the built-in expectations of an EVA incentive system. Voluntarily assumed by managers, the targets are in fact rarely achieved, but the exertions lift performance beyond seemingly realistic aspirations. The combination of EVA and stretch had produced results that lifted SPX's share price from $15.375 in January 1996, soon after Blystone took over, to

$70.8125 eighteen months later. That record made the merger announcement seem realistic.

Indeed, Blystone had done so well at SPX that he soon went on a hunt for an acquisition. In the spring of 1998, he made a hostile bid for Echlin, a large Connecticut auto parts manufacturer, whereupon the Dana Corporation made a better offer and snatched the prize. The situation had its ironies. Blystone planned to boost Echlin's performance by instituting an EVA program similar to the one he had at SPX. He was unaware that Echlin was already implementing EVA.

After his failure at Echlin, Blystone broadened his sights. He told one of the authors that he was not restricting his choices to the auto parts industry. He was in the market for any industrial company that was underperforming and could be turned around by the team that he had put together at SPX. The unstated assumption, of course, was that the price would be right.

The price for General Signal was $45 a share, which came to some $2 billion, plus $335 million of debt that SPX assumed. That $45 per share, to be paid in SPX stock and cash, meant a 19.6 percent premium for General Signal's shareholders, based on the two companies' share prices on the previous trading day. General Signal's owners had the option of exchanging their shares for cash, or SPX stock, or a 60/40 stock–cash combination.

What made that 19.6 percent premium reasonable? Lengthy, detailed analysis by Stern Stewart & Co. (which wrote the prescribed "fairness letter" to SPX) provided the financial rationale. General Signal's past performance was compared with a "peer group" of six companies that, while not exactly comparable, were the closest counterparts that could be found. General Signal had, for some time, been lagging the peer group by several measures, not the least of which was total return to shareholders; it also lagged the S&P 500. Its prospects for the future, according to several analysts, were also behind the peer group. That suggested that the premium was not niggardly.

Most compelling was the analysis of projections of the merged company over the next decade. Both the expected EVA improvements and the free cash-flow projections over that period were discounted to present value. Both methods of valuation give the same result, but the EVA analysis has the advantage of indicating when value is created, year by year. Free cash flow, on the other hand, can be either positive or negative in any year, depending on when investments are made. Discounted cash flow is the more traditional method, but EVA is more revealing.

The results of the exercise: on a per-share basis, the present value of the merged company was $51.04. When anticipated after-tax synergy benefits of $18 million in 1999 and $31 million thereafter were included in the calculation, the per-share value was boosted to $58.77. On the other hand, if the effect of synergies was excluded but a long-term inflation rate of 1 percent a year was assumed, the per-share value would go to $55.11. With a 3 percent annual inflation rate and no synergies, the share value would be $67.37.

Under these circumstances, a price of $45 per share seemed eminently fair to SPX's shareholders. The margin between $45 and the range of higher per-share values indicated that SPX would not be paying an excessive premium. It seemed equally fair to General Signal, given its lackluster performance. It could hardly hope to capture all the expected improvement over 10 years, for then SPX would be denied any reward for its exertions.

Unhappily, the market reacted unfavorably to the merger. On the last trading day before the announcement, SPX closed at $64.50. (It had been as high as $79.06.) After the announcement, the stock began a steady decline and hit a low of $36.06 on October 19, 1998. The only interpretation that could be made was that the market did not buy the logic of the deal. Many observers felt that the two companies were too dissimilar to hold forth the prospect of success, Blystone's optimism notwithstanding. There were other factors as well. The entire market was declining, and the auto parts suppliers—including Federal-Mogul and Dana, as well as SPX—declined even more steeply, as they generally do. Auto parts suppliers tend to be very volatile, both because they are highly leveraged and because they are dependent on the cyclical character of the auto industry.

There was a happy ending, however. After that October low, SPX's share price began an impressive comeback and reached $94 on July 21, 1999—a year and a day after the merger announcement. It then fell back a bit, into the mid-80s, in the late summer and fall. Clearly, the market now thought the merger had been a success. In December, SPX announced that one of its units, Inrange Technologies, had introduced a "fiber channel director" for storage area networks. It caused quite a stir among investors who follow developments in the computer world. SPX's shares went to 122, before falling back; its closing price nearly hit 180 in August 2000 and in mid-November it closed at 118.94.

We turn now to the strategic alliance as an alternative to acquisition. Acquisitions can present extraordinary opportunities for value creation, but they are inherently costly because of the inevitable premiums that have to be paid. Moreover, the deal often involves the acquisition of less attractive businesses as part of the package. The new operations can also be very difficult to integrate into the acquirer's organization because of differences in cultures, financial systems, pay plans, and the like.

What can be achieved expensively through an acquisition can often be gained more cost-effectively through a strategic alliance. Analysis of the viability of a strategic alliance begins with the premise that it takes three things to introduce a product: you've got to design it, make it, and sell it. Many companies automatically assume that they will perform all three of these functions. This is particularly true of old-line industrial companies with a long tradition of vertical integration.

By contrast, the analytical thrust should be: how critical is it for us, as a company, to control all of these functions? Can any of these functions be done better, faster, or with less capital by someone else?

Figure 8.2 represents the basic model for using alliances to support a high-value business strategy. In the center circle is the core business. Strategic alliances and factored products are used to build around the core. Alliances and factored products can be used to fill gaps in product offerings and expand on the core business to complete a company's strategic plan.

Figure 8.2 represents a continuum of control. For the core business, you need to control all three of the functions discussed previously:

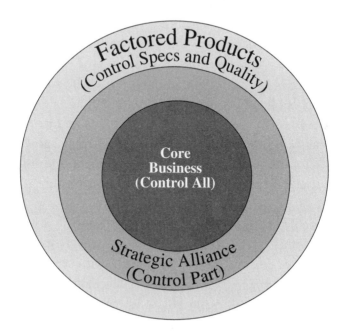

Figure 8.2   **Corporate Business Strategy**

design, manufacturing, and sales. In strategic alliances, represented in the inner ring, there is partial control over these functions. In the outer ring, consisting of factored products, control is exercised only over the specifications and the quality of the product.

The farther away from the core business a project is, the farther into the outer rings you will want the initiative to be. If the products in the outer rings take off, then you may want to pull them into the core either by buying out your partner or otherwise acquiring the technology and the resources that you need to bring them into the core.

It is said that joint ventures are risky. True, but we believe that at times it can be riskier to go it alone. Sole reliance on internal development is inherently risky. There are complex technical requirements, long development cycles, and enormous costs. And a damaging not-invented-here syndrome can develop in a company that isolates itself from outside influences. By contrast, one of the main advantages of a joint venture is that the cost of capital can be shared with another company that has a better capability of spreading the risk of a new venture, especially in foreign deals. EVA analysis can be of great benefit in quantifying the advantages.

Strategic alliances, even failed ones, often have a marvelous side effect in exposing the partners to new markets and to creative and effective approaches to them. It has been said that most joint ventures fail. You have to go beyond that statement and ask: in what sense do they fail? In many cases, a failed joint venture represents a full-blown acquisition or an internal initiative that you did not undertake. So, if you could have done something solely with your own capital, and it ultimately failed when done through an alliance, you avoided a bigger capital hit. In other words, with strategic alliances, you get more chances to roll the dice on development opportunities.

Various forms of strategic alliances can be used to leverage a core business to create value. Each has its own advantages and disadvantages:

- Licensing.
- Contract Development.
- Contract Manufacturing.
- Commercial Agreements (Nonequity Ventures).
- Partial Equity Ventures.
- Joint Ventures.

Licensing is a cheap and often effective way of acquiring the first functional requirement for product introduction: design and development. Contract development involves hiring someone else to do the development work for you, either on a project basis or on a continuing basis. A technology exchange is a form of licensing, except that it is a two-way street and involves some modicum of technical support in addition to the licensing of the relevant technology.

Often, someone else can make something for you cheaper and better, pursuant to a contract manufacturing agreement. Commercial agreements, which are nonequity joint ventures, are very flexible vehicles. Frequently, they involve the third functional requirement—sales and distribution of the product—and they sometimes include elements of design and manufacturing functions.

With a partial equity venture, you put your money where your mouth is. You take a minority equity position in the partner company, and you often enter into some kind of marketing arrangement where you distribute the product. A full equity joint venture is the whole enchilada. Let us briefly review the major benefits and shortcomings of these various types of alliances.

Licensing

Through licensing, you can achieve access to proven technology, reduce your financial exposure, and more easily redirect development efforts as the market changes. It helps you expand your product lines. The disadvantages are clear. The technology is not proprietary, and you can lose control. Your licensing partner can go off in a totally different direction, and application knowledge is an issue. Sometimes, a licensing agreement is combined with an agreement involving know-how transfer, and that can be an effective way to deal with the application-knowledge disadvantage of pure licensing.

Contract Development

If access to talent isn't available in-house, or if your current R&D department is overloaded, you can buy some R&D through a contract development arrangement. It is an excellent solution for businesses that occasionally find themselves in a technology crisis. Developing a network of good R&D shops is a marvelous way to deliver value. The main disadvantage of contract development is that it is very difficult to manage because you don't really control it, and there is no immediate access to application experience. Also, it raises issues of confidentiality and doesn't contribute to the development of your internal talent.

Contract Manufacturing

Contract manufacturing is commonly used by athletic-shoe companies and toy companies, which, if they had proprietary production facilities, would be buried by capital costs attributable to unpredictable and sometimes short-run items, such as Michael Jordan sneakers and Cabbage Patch Dolls. Advantages are significant: avoidance of prohibitive capacity costs, minimized capital calls, access to manufacturers with varied capabilities in terms of operations, and lower labor costs. Much of this kind of work is done in developing countries such as Mexico and the emerging markets in Asia, though the garment industries in the United States have long employed contract shops. Often, your partner has an ability that you lack and can take on business that is counterseasonal or counter-cyclical to what you do, or can more effectively absorb overhead and capital costs. The disadvantages are a loss of proprietary manufac-turing skills, which can be a competitive advantage, and less control over the manufacturing process. There can also be a public relations hazard, if third-world contractors can be plausibly charged with running sweatshops.

Commercial Agreements

When projects involve joint product development and marketing in a commercial venture, the parties often carve up the design, development, manufacturing, and marketing responsibilities by agreement, without significant equity investment. An example would be the Visa, AT&T, and airline credit-card alliances. In ef-fect, you are attempting to take advantage of the partner's inherent integrating efficiencies without a substantial investment in capital and people. This can also be an effective vehicle for cashing out of an unprofitable product line without losing total control. Again, the disadvantages are the issues of control and exclusivity.

To demonstrate the operation of a nonequity commercial al-liance, we will use an example from the Allen-Bradley/Rockwell Automation experience. It involved Allen-Bradley and IBM form-ing a commercial alliance to produce a factory-hardened personal computer. As you may know, Allen-Bradley/Rockwell Automation is a world leader in factory floor automation. IBM is the standard for office-based personal computers.

By the early 1980s, the use of PCs on the factory floor was be-coming widespread. The generation of PCs used at that time did not survive the operating environment of a factory very well. IBM had credibility in personal computers; Allen-Bradley had credibility on the factory floor. There was an enormous projected capital cost for

Allen-Bradley to develop its own proprietary PC. The idea was to take an IBM PC, harden it for factory use, and then market it under the joint logos of IBM and Allen-Bradley.

Allen-Bradley was able to develop a commercially viable product with almost no capital investment, but, in the long run, the market for factory-hardened PCs fell short of expectations. There were a couple of reasons. The machines were very expensive, so some users bought cheap PCs instead and replaced them after a year or two. Also, the durability of standard PCs improved; then, with the onset of networks, people were able to put the PCs into environments that were less rigorous. But Allen-Bradley/Rockwell avoided an enormous capital cost by partnering with IBM—and learned a lot about marketing PCs for the factory as part of integrated automation systems.

Partial Equity Alliances

This type of alliance involves a partial equity investment in the partner, coupled with some kind of product commercialization arrangement. Often, this involves a mom-and-pop shop for which a major industry player provides capital and, in exchange, gets the exclusive right to market the partner's product. The capital investment is generally needed because most of these companies are entrepreneurial and are chronically strapped.

The advantages: you get rapid access to technology, at a lower cost, obviously, than in an acquisition. You can hedge evolving strategies; you can roll the dice on several of these for the capital cost of one acquisition. And if the technology gains acceptance, you can bring it closer to the core by acquiring additional equity or completely buying out the partner. Partial equity alliances are most often used when a large, well-heeled company with excellent distribution capabilities hooks up with an emerging technology company. Disadvantages again involve control. Also, the interests of the parties may diverge.

We can demonstrate the operation of a partial equity alliance with another example from the Allen-Bradley/Rockwell experience. By the mid-1980s, there was a growing interest, on the factory floor, in the use of what are called color graphic panels. These are interactive panels with screen monitors that illustrate things that are actually occurring on the factory floor. Gould Modicon, an Allen-Bradley/Rockwell competitor, announced a new color graphics panel for future delivery. Allen-Bradley had forecast a capital call of at least $2.5 million for internal development of a similar product.

The strategy Allen-Bradley devised to deal with the competitive threat and pursue an opportunity at the same time was to hook up with a company already in the business, obtain exclusive sales and distribution rights, and cooperatively develop the second generation of color graphics products. This strategy was implemented by acquiring a 25 percent interest in Dyanpro Systems, Inc., of Vancouver, which was an established player in the industry. Allen-Bradley/Rockwell was ultimately able to buy the entire business by March 1999. This turned out to be the front end of an enormously successful business venture for what is now known as Rockwell Automation. The company does not report segment data for this business, but sales of display panels by Rockwell Automation are now estimated to exceed $50 million a year, and this product provides an excellent return for Rockwell's high-margin systems business.

Joint Ventures

The advantages of entering into a full-fledged equity joint venture include full sharing of technology; market entry and application knowledge; high asset utilization; and integrating efficiencies with the partner. The primary disadvantage is that it requires significant formalities in management. You have to be capable of melding sometimes very diverse cultures if you are talking about a full-scale joint venture, and that is really difficult.

Disadvantages of joint ventures include the need to share profitability. There may evolve a divergence of the partners' strategic interests, and the venture can be difficult to unwind if the partners do not achieve their intended goals. A good way to overcome these shortcomings is to put in effective unwind provisions at the front end.

Briggs & Stratton's joint venture in China offers some insights into the elements of a value-producing joint venture. By the mid-1980s, the U.S. demand for durable cast iron engines, an old-line technology, was eroding. But there was a continuing demand in developing countries. China is a diesel-dominated market for outdoor power equipment, and Briggs & Stratton wanted to push the Chinese market more toward gas-engine technologies. The company had all the existing cast iron engine production assets in Milwaukee, and the mayor and party boss of Chongqing, China, were very interested in a commercial engine venture. So the strategy was to move the cast iron engine operating assets to Chongqing. The joint venture would produce 10- and 16-hp engines, and the engines were to be sold in China and worldwide by Briggs & Stratton.

This joint venture was incorporated as a 52-24-24 percent joint venture, with Puling Machinery Works of Chongqing and Yimin, a large defense contractor, as the partners. Control is an issue in China when you are trying to get things done. So, Briggs & Stratton took an extra couple of percentage points in this one.

The EVA results were remarkable until the 1997–1998 Asian crisis. Briggs & Stratton was annually receiving a hard currency dividend of around $1.6 million on a capital investment of about $4 million, and much of that capital was a transfer of assets that would have been rationalized in the absence of the venture.

A few basic points should be made on how to approach the design and implementation of strategic alliances. It is said that most of them do not succeed. Well, that is correct. Most of the time, you roll the dice at the craps table and it doesn't pay off big. But if you roll the dice consistently enough, with a high enough potential for a payoff and a minimum capital investment, the EVA gain can be substantial.

An acquaintance who was a deal guy at Pillsbury once told us that joint ventures are like marriages, except there is no sex to relieve the tension. If you are impatient or you have a control fetish, you shouldn't be doing them. You must have realistic expectations for any integrating efficiencies, and choose partners who have a set of values and beliefs that are similar to your own. You can't get heavy-handed with your partner. Often, you also have to handle the dynamic of the smaller partner dealing with the big nasty Fortune 500 corporation; you have to work that through. Nonetheless, the EVA rewards in strategic alliances can be hefty and are well worth the diplomatic exertions.

Chapter 9

EVA Incentives

We revert now to a subject that was dealt with briefly in Chapter 2. Nothing, it can fairly be claimed, is more important to a successful EVA implementation than a carefully designed EVA incentive program. An EVA measurement system without a comparable incentive plan is, in the long run, doomed to failure because employees will be rewarded for achieving goals that may be at cross-purposes with EVA. If you are measuring corporate performance by EVA but rewarding executives, say, on gains in earnings per share, there is an obvious conflict. EPS is not only a poor measurement tool because of accounting distortions, as pointed out in Chapter 1, but it can be manipulated to produce favorable results that, in EVA terms, are anything but favorable. Nonetheless, we know of one large EVA company in the Midwest with an executive compensation plan half-based on EVA and half on EPS.

We also argued that return on investment (ROI) and return on net assets (RONA), frequent criteria for executive bonuses, are flawed. Thus, it makes no sense to put the company on EVA and have executives incentivized by schemes whose only merit is that they are traditional. Many bonus plans are based on improvements in operating earnings. This is a particularly pernicious arrangement, for operating earnings take no account of the cost of capital. One sure way to increase operating profits is to invest heavily to increase sales and market share, with no regard to the impact on EVA. Executives on any of these plans will be torn between personal pecuniary interest and the furtherance of shareholder value that EVA represents.

On occasion, top management is eager to adopt EVA before it is politic to install an EVA compensation plan. That occurred when Fred Butler introduced the EVA discipline in The Manitowoc Company in 1991. His purpose, as detailed in Chapter 5, was to impose a desperately needed restraint on the use of capital. He was able to do that on his own authority but felt that he could not go to the board of directors for an EVA incentive plan at that time, inasmuch as a new bonus plan had recently been adopted.

The new capital stringency worked, for Butler put all the authority of his office behind it. The board was impressed and, within a relatively short time, voted in an EVA bonus plan. But this two-step process is not recommended. Sometimes, there is concern that the new EVA plan will mean an immediate shortfall in executive compensation, and the consequences to morale are dismaying. A company will then put a floor under the first year's EVA bonus by using the old formula. This does no great harm, so long as it is limited to one year.

Traditional incentive plans have other deficiencies, apart from being grounded on the wrong criteria. They are typically based on the achievement of budgetary goals for the following year, with the goals determined by a lengthy bargaining process. Managers try to keep the goals within limits that they regard as "realistic"—that is to say, not overly ambitious, and well within the capacity of their group. Their supervisors press them to agree to bigger numbers, and there is a lot of pulling and hauling. After the budgets are set, managers are frequently cautious about not exceeding them to any significant degree, which would indicate that the goals were unrealistic in the first instance. Moreover, bonuses are often "capped," which would eliminate any incentive for extraordinary performance.

EVA incentive plans are entirely different. They are not set annually in a lengthy negotiation, but are fixed in advance for a three- or five-year period, after study at the highest corporate level—generally, with technical consultation with outside experts. Moreover, EVA bonuses are "uncapped" and thus, if the company is successful, they amount to a far higher proportion of total compensation than is achieved under traditional bonus plans. Obviously, there is quite a difference in incentive if one can realistically increase one's pay by 50 percent or 60 percent as compared to 10 percent or 15 percent in a traditional plan. An abiding problem in most American industries (it is worse abroad) is that fixed pay is much too high a proportion of total compensation. This system puts no premium on innovation and risk taking.

The essence of an EVA incentive plan is that it promotes the goal of increasing shareholder value, to which the measurement program and the entire EVA management system are dedicated. The target is the annual "expected EVA improvement," the achievement of which will bring 100 percent of the "target bonus." That target bonus, in turn, is a percentage of the employee's annual salary, ranging from 100 percent for the CEO down, typically, to 10 percent for the lowest-ranking employee in the program. The virtue of the uncapped plan is that the target bonus will be exceeded if the EVA improvement exceeds its target by a stipulated amount, known as the "interval." Thus, if the EVA improvement target is 100 and the interval is 50, and the achievement is 150, the total bonus is double the target bonus. If the total achievement is 200, the bonus is tripled.

But there is also downside risk. If the EVA achievement falls short of the target for the year, the target bonus is shaved. Typically, a 50 percent shortfall will bring only 50 percent of the stipulated bonus; a greater shortfall generally means no bonus at all. And if the year's results show a decline in EVA, the accrued bonuses that employees have received will be debited.

But how can prior bonuses be debited? The answer is an escrow account known as the bonus bank. There are two main types. In one, the target bonus is paid out in cash, but one-third of the "excess bonus" is banked; in later years, negative performance results in debits to the bank, but one-third of any remaining sums is distributed, year by year. This means that managers always have some prior earnings at risk, which tends to squelch any impulse to "game" the system by inflating one year's results at the expense of the future. Everything is designed to induce long-term thinking.

The other type is the "all-in" bonus bank. The entire bonus is placed in the bank, with one-third to be drawn down each year; again, negative performance brings debits. The advantage of this system is that participants have far more at risk, from the outset—the entire bonus, not merely the "excess bonus." Thus, if the target bonus is achieved in the first year, the payout is only one-third rather than 100 percent. (The plan is prefunded, to have something in the kitty.) In the second year, if the target bonus is earned, the payout is again one-third, but it is one-third of the larger, accrued sum—and so on for successive years. The downside risk in the "all-in" bank is also greater for another reason: if the first year has negative results, the bank starts out with a debit. With the other type of bonus bank, there is simply no payout.

To illustrate how the EVA incentive compensation system works, let's look at the Briggs & Stratton plan, in operation since 1993, and discuss the type of behavior the program is intended to encourage. The plan sets annual performance goals—the expected EVA improvement—and target incentive bonuses that together determine the payouts for the year. Target bonuses for key executives range from 20 percent to 80 percent of base salary, depending on the executive's position. An executive's actual bonus may be more or less than this target, but the final amount depends largely on whether the EVA performance goals are achieved by the corporation overall and by that particular executive's operating division. (Bonuses for executives at the corporate level are totally dependent on corporate results.)

For a typical divisional executive at Briggs & Stratton, 50 percent of his incentive bonus is based on the corporate EVA performance factor, 40 percent is based on the divisional performance factor, and 10 percent is based on the individual performance factor. The individual performance factor is a number ranging from 0 to 1.5 and is based on achievement of a goal in the executive's area of responsibility. For a quality control executive, this might mean getting certification of a particular plant or division; for a purchasing executive, it might be achieving a specified cost reduction target in parts purchased. The following calculation illustrates how the system works.

Assumptions

Participant: Divisional General Manager (Target bonus: 35 percent of base pay)

Base Salary: $100,000

Corporate Performance Factor (CPF): 1.1 (slightly above target)

Divisional Performance Factor (DPF): 0.9 (slightly below target)

Individual Performance Factor (IPF): 1.5 (maximum target)

Calculation

$$
\begin{aligned}
\text{EVA Bonus} &= (\text{Salary} \times \text{Target \%} \times \text{CPF}) \times 50\% \\
&\quad (\text{Salary} \times \text{Target \%} \times \text{DPF}) \times 40\% \\
&\quad (\text{Salary} \times \text{Target \%} \times \text{IPF}) \times 10\% \\
&= (\$100,000 \times 35\% \times 1.1) \times 50\% \\
&\quad (\$100,000) \times 35\% \times .9) \times 40\% \\
&\quad (\$100,000) \times 35\% \times 1.5) \times 10\% \\
&= \$19,250 + \$12,600 + \$5,250 \\
&= \$37,100
\end{aligned}
$$

In the Briggs & Stratton plan, if the target bonus is exceeded, any amount over 125 percent of the targeted figure is "banked." (Plans vary in the threshold for banking.) Then, as in most plans with this type of bank, in any given year, one-third of any positive balance in the bank is paid out. If there is a "negative bonus" in any year, the balance in the bank is reduced by that amount.

In addition to bonuses based on EVA, a significant portion of total compensation for key executives at Briggs & Stratton is tied directly to stock performance. We are referring to leveraged stock options (LSOs), briefly mentioned in Chapter 2. Awarded to those "senior executives"—primarily corporate officers—who are responsible for the overall results of the company, these options are designed to reward key employees when the company's stock performs exceptionally well, thereby providing them with an additional incentive to maximize that performance. But LSOs differ in one important respect from conventional stock options, which are generally granted with an exercise price equal to the current market price. LSOs, by contrast, have an exercise price that rises each year by an amount equal to the firm's cost of capital (adjusted, as shown below, for dividends and illiquidity). This steadily rising exercise price is designed to ensure that, if the stock price does not produce at least a cost-of-capital return for the option period, the options are worthless. Thus, executives cannot benefit unless shareholders receive the minimum return on their investment to which they are entitled.

The LSO program is linked to the company's EVA bonus plan in that the number of options granted in a given year is directly related to the EVA bonus payout for the year. Once a bonus amount has been determined, each executive receives, in addition to the cash bonus, out-of-the-money options on company stock. The amount of stock is generous—far more shares are awarded than in conventional plans. The number of optioned shares is determined by a calculation that produces a total dollar value of shares under option equal to 10 times the amount of the EVA bonus. (Multiply the bonus by 10, divide by the share price, and you get the number of shares). Hence the term "leveraged" stock options.

This means that, each year, a senior executive effectively receives double the EVA bonus, with the requirement that the additional chunk be invested in a 10-to-1 leveraged stock investment. This matching grant approach allows the executive to avoid current income tax liability on the "reinvested" portion of the bonus.

The final piece of the incentive-equation puzzle is determining the exercise price at which the LSOs will be in-the-money. The aim here is to reward only stock performance that exceeds the minimum acceptable return to shareholders, so executives should profit only from exceptional performance. Therefore, the LSOs go in-the-money only if the company's stock returns provide at least a "deemed" cost-of-capital return over the option period.

Under the plan, the deemed cost of capital is calculated by taking the risk-free interest rate (the current rate on 30-year U.S. Treasury Bonds), adding a market equity risk premium (historically, about 6 percent for companies of average risk), and then subtracting both the anticipated annual percentage dividend yield and a risk factor to compensate executives for the illiquidity and the lack of diversification associated with the options. At the time it adopted the LSO program, for example, Briggs & Stratton had an anticipated annual dividend yield over the option period of about 3 percent. Therefore, assuming a 7 percent risk-free rate at the time of the grant, the deemed cost of capital return would be as follows:

30-year U.S. Bond Rate (7 percent)
+ Equity Risk Premium (6 percent) – Deemed Dividend (3 percent)
– Risk Factor (Illiquid and Undiversified: 2 percent) = 8 percent

Because the latter three elements of this equation are assumed to remain constant over the option period, the only variable that changes is the risk-free rate. Therefore, we can state that, in effect, the cost of capital is the 30-year U.S. bond rate plus 1 percent.

Under this plan, top managers will not get a penny from their LSOs until they have provided a minimum return that, except for the aforementioned adjustments, equals the company's cost of capital. But if they exceed their shareholders' expectations and provide them with an exceptional return, the leveraging structure of LSOs ensures that executives will be very well rewarded.

Ultimately, as previously suggested, management's long-term performance is best measured by Market Value Added (MVA), the amount by which the market value of the firm exceeds the capital invested in it. LSOs contribute effectively to this MVA imperative by offering strong incentives. Of course, all equity-based incentives are flawed in the sense that many factors beyond management's influence end up driving market value; and this in turn means that, for any given period, the payoff from LSOs could result from good luck as much as good performance. But we believe that an executive's effectiveness in responding to uncontrollable events is a fundamental aspect of value creation. The market's response to negative and positive uncontrollable events will ebb and flow. Therefore, an executive who effectively plays the cards being dealt will show a superior MVA over time.

For example, Briggs & Stratton's primary business of supplying engines for lawn and garden equipment is intensely seasonal, and this seasonal variability is further exacerbated by weather patterns. These factors are out of management's control. There are two basic ways to manage this uncertainty while meeting the demands of this market. One is to build enormous amounts of inventory on a relatively level schedule (the "high working capital" solution). The other is to hold down inventories while developing the capability to ramp up production in a hurry (the "chase" strategy), which involves higher operating capital and employee redundancy costs. Creative value managers are most effective in analyzing which of these approaches, or combinations thereof, will deliver the highest EVA, given the competitive environment. Tactics such as creative plant architecture and alternative workforces will give managers a "value edge" in dealing with the uncontrollable aspects of their business.

An odd though not uncommon criticism of EVA is that there is too much focus on short-term performance. It is well known that the value of any capital asset is the present value of the future cash flow that can be derived from it. And, of course, the mechanics of calculating present value assign higher value (by using lower discount rates) to cash flows produced in the here and now. But doing well in the short run does not preclude doing well in the long run. For most EVA companies that we have studied, long-term value tends to be achieved through consistent and sustained annual increases in EVA performance. The incentives that we have described—banked bonuses and LSOs—promote both ends. As in the Briggs & Stratton LSO plan, the right to participate in long-term appreciation is earned only by maintaining near-term capital efficiency. And, although the need to make trade-offs between this year's and future EVA will certainly arise (this, after all, is the meaning of "investment"), management's challenge is to keep its eye on both targets at once.

There are naysayers, of course. Executives of companies that have experienced significant revenue growth, but less-than-splendid stock performance, often voice the criticism that value management is biased against growth and innovation, and that the EVA discipline forces capital to be "managed down" in pursuit of maximum return. One should not be surprised to learn, however, that most of these companies have at-the-money option programs with constant exercise prices. Such option programs, restive shareholders ultimately learn, can provide handsome returns to executives employing maintenance or revenue growth strategies, even when they fail to deliver on shareholders' demands for a cost of capital return.

Under an EVA incentive plan, by contrast, the company and/or relevant division must achieve its EVA target for managers to receive bonus rewards in any given year. But remember that a portion of such awards is banked and is subject to loss if EVA returns fall in future years, thus limiting any temptation management might have to cut back on necessary investment. Consider also that the annual EVA bonus determines the number of LSOs that are granted. And LSOs are likely to be a powerful motivator for growth—though only profitable growth—because they amplify the risks and rewards for management. The reason: any improvement in EVA that investors think will be sustained will be capitalized into the value of the shares; for example, a company with a cost of capital of 10 percent that increases its EVA by $1 million will see its value appreciate by $10 million. This leveraging effect makes LSOs a potent way to get management to concentrate on building EVA over the long haul.

In other words, an EVA incentive plan provides strong motivation for growth combined with capital discipline. For those companies with significant growth opportunities, EVA will impel managers to pursue both top-line growth and efficiency. "Managing down" capital will maximize the payout opportunity only in situations calling for contraction of the business or liquidation.

Now, what about the cost of LSOs to shareholders, commonly calculated by the Black–Scholes–Merton formula (discussed at length in Chapter 11). The LSOs issued by Briggs & Stratton to its senior executives at the beginning of 1995 had a Black–Scholes disclosure value of only 14.8 percent of the then-current stock price. By contrast, an at-the-money option with similar terms would have been valued for disclosure purposes at 25.1 percent of the current stock price—because of the greater likelihood that the options would be exercised. That means that far more LSOs can be granted to executives for the same shareholder cost.

When this premium option program replaced a prior at-the-money program at Briggs & Stratton, the initial response from some quarters of the senior executive group was somewhat less than enthusiastic. But that initial reaction soon gave way to a good deal of excitement because Briggs's stock, less than three years into the program, had risen to within a few dollars of the exercise price. Still, a company considering this type of program should be aware that "retention risk"—the curious phrase that means the risk of not retaining employees—is a real issue, particularly when there are plenty of companies out there offering conventional at-the-money or even discounted options.

On the other hand, keeping a certain amount of retention risk may not necessarily be a bad thing. The premium option approach can help redefine the character of the executive group. For those managers who are confident of their ability to deliver above-average performance, the potential rewards are very great—and they are the ones most likely to stick around under an EVA plan. To attract and keep management talent optimistic about their ability to deliver high-value growth, LSOs may well be the ticket.

Moreover, the cost to shareholders is not great. There is much less dilution with LSOs than with standard options, for the LSOs can only be exercised at a price that rises each year—which means that the company has to do exceedingly well for the options to be worth anything. If that happens, the shareholders will be so bountifully rewarded that they could well afford the dilution involved. By contrast, regular options—given out more broadly—have a fixed exercise price and are far more likely to be in the money if the company succeeds.

The specific design of the Briggs & Stratton plan will not be suitable for all companies. Introducing an effective EVA incentive program requires a careful review of the distinctive competitive and operational challenges faced by the particular company, and then tailoring the program accordingly. To be most effective, some of the features of the LSOs discussed here may require adaptation or phase-in timetables. Consider a small drug company with great potential but with most of its key products still under review by the

FDA. In this case, you would probably want to modify the requirement that LSOs can be earned only through EVA improvement,
which might take some time to arrive.

Moreover, for plant-level incentive programs, you would probably want to base the incentive on performance that is more within
the control of the manager or employees, such as plant-level EVA.
At the level of the shop floor, you should also consider basing some
part of the incentive on specific "value drivers," such as capital
equipment efficiency, inventory management, or labor productivity.
In short, there is no cookie-cutter program. A successful effort requires not only a thorough understanding of the dynamics of value
creation, but the input of a company's most insightful managers. In
that way, you can shape an organization where everyone knows
what they are paid to do.

Chapter 10

How EVA Can Fail

What motivated that CEO to announce his retirement a year in advance? Perhaps he wanted to assure would-be successors that he was not planning to stay indefinitely. Whatever his motives, his premature announcement was for a time a body blow to the EVA implementation that had been underway for six months; in another three months, the EVA incentive system was supposed to go into effect. Nonetheless, after the CEO's announcement, the head of human resources, a key player in any EVA implementation, stopped going to meetings of the steering committee, the topside company committee responsible for putting the program into place.

Then other members of the committee visibly lost their enthusiasm for the project. After all, they had been comfortable under the old system of negotiated annual bonus targets, under which they had personally prospered. Why risk the uncertainty of the new EVA incentives if the CEO, who had started the experiment, was soon to leave?

In the end, disaster was averted, though it was a close call. The CEO forcefully reasserted his authority, announcing that the new program would go into effect in three months as planned, while he was still very much in control. He realized that he had little choice, for he had previously publicized the fact that the company was going on EVA. It would have been monumentally embarrassing to reverse course now, particularly since the company was planning a large public share offering.

The incident illustrates one of the prime causes of EVA failure—the lack, or the perceived lack, of full support from a company's chief executive. At this point, the reader might wonder why we are talking about failure. The previous chapters have laid out in detail the road map to success. But our discussion would hardly be complete without mention of the hazards that can subvert a program, or of the unfavorable environments in which it would be impossible for EVA to survive, let alone flourish.

Without question, the attitude of the chief executive is the primary determinant of the success or failure of the program. During the past four or five years, as the program was becoming widely known, a company occasionally adopted EVA largely for public relations purposes. Many security analysts regard the embrace of EVA as a big plus, and there have been occasions—as with the Olin Corporation a few years ago, and with Federal-Mogul in 1997—when the mere announcement of an EVA plan caused a rise in the share price. But if the chief executive's support for the effort is less than wholehearted, the program is doomed to failure. The reason: EVA is such a radical departure from the traditional way of measuring success and motivating people that it requires unremitting pressure from the top to enforce compliance in the echelons below. We must not forget that the adoption of EVA is synonymous with a total change in culture: size for its own sake, market share, and so-called top line growth are out; value is in. Discipline in rejecting acquisitions and other investments that are deemed too expensive is crucial.

As suggested earlier, change is always stressful and often threatening in a mature bureaucracy. Unless there is a sense of urgency created by a desperate situation, most people are loath to tamper with settled practice. The nature of a rut is that it is often comfortable, and many executives have been enriched by following its well-worn grooves. The one person who can shatter accepted practice, insist on change, and enforce change is the chief executive. Normally, the CEO cannot singlehandedly adopt EVA. Board action is invariably encouraged, if not required, to install a new incentive plan, but thereafter the fate of the program is in the CEO's hands.

EVA can fail for other reasons, as we shall see, but it is doomed to failure unless the CEO leads the charge. What does this require? The CEO must not only be on the steering committee (other members should include the chief financial officer, the chief operating officer, and other key operating executives) but should chair the committee. Not as a referee, for the committee is not a parliamentary body, but as the champion of the program, coordinating the discussion, resolving conflicts, and enforcing the timetable for action.

There are circumstances in which EVA's prospects are dim and it would be prudent not even to make the effort, if the facts are known in advance. One such circumstance is where the top executives of a company are overpaid for poor performance, so that it would be extremely likely that they would earn less under an EVA bonus plan. A few years back, Stern Stewart was called in to make a presentation to a large corporation which, under threat of a hostile takeover, had defensively bought a pharmaceutical company. The buyer was unacquainted with both the drug business and the quality of the talent running the company, and thus kept everybody on with signing bonuses and long-term contracts. When Stern Stewart tried to explain in its presentation how EVA would improve total corporate performance, it immediately encountered a frosty response along the lines of "This would never work in our culture." The naysayers were quite correct. Under an EVA incentive program, the top executives would unquestionably earn less.

Mediocre talent in the executive suite also bodes ill for a successful EVA effort. To use a baseball analogy, Stern Stewart's star coaches cannot make .320 hitters out of .220 hitters. If one tries, an unsuccessful implementation is the certain result. The problem is that if you put somebody on an EVA program, the rewards are tied to substantive improvement in performance. But what if these people are not capable of delivering it because their personal skills are just not up to the task? Then the EVA missionaries are in the position of setting unattainable goals, and the certain result will be frustration for everybody concerned.

A fourth cause of failure, far more common than the previous two, is an uncongenial corporate culture, characteristic of an old-line public utility or of a state-owned company or government department. In these entities, jobs are often sinecures, and promotion is often more dependent on seniority than on merit. In that kind of setting, people are unaccustomed to variable pay, unless it is negotiated, and they do not enjoy the prospect of being objectively measured by a rigorous standard like EVA. They are also psychologically accustomed to an unstressful office routine, where punctuality is prized at both ends of the day. After hearing an EVA presentation, one executive exclaimed, "With that program, we'd have to be here until 6 P.M. every night!" Only a strong chief executive, determined to impose EVA, can overcome that kind of resistance. But it can be done, as Marvin Runyon showed at the U.S. Postal Service, and there have been other examples abroad.

In European countries, EVA has had to overcome stiff resistance to gain acceptance. Despite its adoption by such well-known companies as Diageo, Siemens, Tate & Lyle, Lafarge, and International Service Systems, it is still an uphill battle, not to win an initial hearing but to overcome a wall of skepticism and a lack of responsiveness to the key concepts that bring applause in the United States. Sizable cultural differences explain the problem.

Stern Stewart learned that lesson in France a few years ago. Early in 1997, it was on the brink of signing up three companies that seemed eager to adopt EVA to become more competitive in the new global economy. Then President Jacques Chirac suddenly called a parliamentary election and, to everyone's surprise, the socialist Lionel Jospin won. Soon thereafter, the three companies had a change of heart about EVA. "The pressure is off us; we no longer have a sense of urgency," one executive confessed, obviously expecting a socialist government to stress the social contract rather than the need for competitive vigor. Another explained, "EVA is in conflict with our mind-set. We don't want people always incentivized by money."

This was a disappointment but not a great surprise. For years, EVA has been a cultural affront to many people in Germany and France, especially in France. Stern Stewart has had great difficulty in talking about any aspect of incentive compensation. Executives are cool to any method of objective evaluation of the performance of individuals and teams; value enhancement as a corporate goal tends to be an alien concept. Employees are not attracted to the notion of having a stake in the company that leads them to act like owners. They have no desire to be owners, with all the risk that entails; they regard themselves as senior claimants, senior liability holders, who take no risks. What is important to them is the size of the unit that a manager oversees, for size determines responsibility, and the level of responsibility determines salary and pension. It is a system that by and large perpetuates the status quo, though there are individuals and companies that are exceptions.

In 1998, Pascal Luciani, then an MBA candidate at the London Business School, produced an interesting paper exploring the cultural impediments facing EVA in Europe. "EVA in Europe—A Cultural Perspective" was based on extensive interviews with businesspeople in several countries, as well as a review of the literature. Luciani concluded that EVA had to overcome tough obstacles to win acceptance. The problem was that companies were not focused on increasing shareholder value by employing capital efficiently. Instead, their emphasis was on growth almost for its own sake, increasing market share, and, in some cases, producing superior products. Companies tended to take their social responsibilities seriously, finding it easier at times to talk more about the interests of stakeholders than those of shareholders. At the same time, managers were not primarily motivated by financial incentives. Instead, they were interested in status, power, and control of ever-larger entities, with the privilege of issuing diktats to subordinates. There was no place in the scheme of things for American-style participatory management.

Luciani presented his survey findings under the rubrics of mind-set, motivation, measurement, and management, and gave examples of each from three countries—France, Germany, and the United Kingdom. Under mind-set, he listed for Germany the belief that "Superior product through advanced engineering brings superior profits," as well as "Concerned with remaining #1 economic power in Europe," and "What's good for the community is good for business"—a thought echoed by the French entry: "Business exists for the good of society." All of these estimable philosophic observations are far from a recognition that the *sine qua non* of corporate success is increasing returns for shareholders.

The primary findings under motivation were similar for all three countries. Germans were motivated by "opportunity for self-actualization and personal development" as well as "lifetime work stability." The French wanted "recognition and respect of peers," together with a "long-term career position." As for the lure of monetary reward, the respondents were remarkably disdainful in all three countries. French managers were reported to believe that "the capitalist philosophy of using monetary incentive to incite initiative and economic performance is . . . an affront." The British were not insulted but were reported to feel "apathy towards discrepancy in pay. Monetary reward is seen as coming automatically with grade or position."

The standards for measuring corporate performance could only dismay anyone who believes in EVA. In Germany, the "focus is on creating long-term profitability" without any reference to the consumption of capital. In all countries, management style is characterized as "strongly influenced by a need for control."

With a cultural atmosphere so different from that in the United States, how was EVA to win any converts? Luciani's basic approach is to avoid any emphasis on monetary incentives but demonstrate how EVA could enhance productive efficiency, a goal of great importance to the Germans, and show how it could enhance, not dilute, managers' control. He would not abandon the EVA incentive plan, but would bring it in through the back door, stressing how EVA would buttress the position of managers, strengthening their powers and enhancing their status. Shareholders as well as stakeholders would benefit, but the interest of shareholders would not be highlighted.

Luciani's paper is useful as an analysis of the problem, though his solution may sound overly cynical. Stressing how EVA can improve productive efficiency and managerial control may be useful as a sales pitch—the wedge under the door, as it were—but it would be impossible to implement a successful EVA program without the spur of monetary rewards at the end of the day. Several European companies, as already mentioned, have understood the point and adopted a full EVA program.

Nor do the comments of Luciani's respondents prove that they are indifferent to the uses of money. Many of them do receive variable pay—bonuses—though the proportion of variable pay to total compensation is much less than in the United States, and it is usually capped at modest levels of performance. But the Europeans clearly think that emphasizing money is indelicate, *infra dig*, gauche, the sort of behavior that can be expected from uncouth Americans.

Moreover, hefty bonuses can represent a public relations problem. British executives do not want to be denounced as "fat cats" in the tabloid press. The solution, as well, can involve a PR gloss, emphasizing how the prosperity of a corporation redounds to the benefit of the community. And more than a PR gloss is involved here. The statement is true.

Chapter 11

New Frontiers: Real Options and Forward-Looking EVA

We now move into territory that has not been fully mapped. Real options, a relatively new concept, can be used in all industries and are of vital importance in the extractive industries—oil and gas, and all manner of mining. Real options theory can also help explain the huge capitalizations of Internet stocks and other high-fliers.

But what, readers might well ask, are real options? The short answer is that they are options on all sorts of future business opportunities—developing an oil field, putting up a plant, indeed all kinds of capital expenditures and strategic decisions. Real options are analogous to the more familiar financial options and are valued basically with the same formula.

A financial option confers the right—but not the obligation—to buy or sell something at a stipulated price. You buy a call option on a share of the XYZ Corporation at $30. If the stock rises above $30 before the expiration date of the option, you exercise it to buy the stock—or, you can sell your option, and your profit would be the spread between \$30 and whatever is the market price. If the stock never reaches \$30, you simply lose the price of the option, which may be only \$2 or \$3 a share. Thus, an option has limited downside risk but much more potential profit because the stock can rise far more than the cost of the option. Options, however, are significantly riskier than common stock, because of the much greater variability of returns.

For over two decades, financial options have been priced according to the Black–Scholes–Merton model, which won Scholes and Merton a Nobel prize (Black died before the honor was conferred). The equations, too complex for these pages, take account of five elements: (1) the stock price, (2) the exercise price, (3) the duration of the option, (4) the risk-free interest rate, and (5) the volatility of the stock. In an upgraded version of the model, there is a sixth item—the dividend yield that is forgone by not buying the stock immediately. The figure for volatility is of great importance: The more volatile the security, the more the option is worth. This may seem paradoxical, but it is logical; there is a greater chance of hitting the exercise price with a stock that bounces up and down a lot than with one that moves sluggishly. And, longer options are worth more than shorter ones because there is more time to hit the target before the expiration date.

Similar elements determine the value of a real option. The duration of the option is the time available before a decision has to be made. The risk-free interest rate plays the same role in both types of options. Instead of a stock price, the present value of the future developed project is plugged in. The exercise price is represented by the cost of the ultimate project, once the decision is made to go forward. A volatility figure is derived from the history of similar projects in the past. The forgone dividend yield is paralleled by a figure for "value leakage" (the value forgone by not investing immediately). If the project is abandoned by the deadline for decision, the only cost is that of the option. That cost might be the expense of initial R&D incurred by a pharmaceutical company, or the staff cost of planning the project, or the cash expended to secure an option to buy a piece of property.

Options bring welcome flexibility to corporate planning. A variety of projects can be explored at relatively small cost, and decisions can be deferred until possible outcomes become clearer. Since long before Black–Scholes–Merton, motion picture production companies have been buying bushels of options on books, plays, and even unpublished manuscripts. A company might pay $12,500 or $25,000 for an option to buy the movie rights to a book for, say, $250,000 or $500,000, with the option to run for a year or two. The property would thus be unavailable to competitors, and the company would have the stated time to canvass casting possibilities, see how the proposed movie would fit into its production lineup, and seek financing. The option is often extended if an additional payment is made. Moreover, the movie company would have several, perhaps dozens, of options outstanding, giving it a wide range of choice. Often, an option is bought in a sudden rush of enthusiasm, which quickly fades. And although authors, who might be ignorant of Hollywood's ways, are often disappointed when their options are not taken up, the system is obviously cheaper than it would be if the company had to buy every property outright to keep it from competitors and then spend months deciding whether to produce.

In an article by Peter Coy in its June 7, 1999, issue, *Business Week* reported on an innovative use of real options by the Enron Corporation, an electrical utility company. Enron built three electrical generating plants in Tennessee and Mississippi that were cheaper to construct than state-of-the-art plants, but they were also less efficient. That mattered not at all: The plants, licensed to operate no more than 50 days a year, were to be used only to meet peak demands when the intercompany price of electricity (a commodity bought and sold across the nation's grids) also peaked. *Business Week* reported that, in June 1998, the cost of a megawatt-hour had soared from $40 to an incredible $7,000 for a short period in sections of the Midwest. Anticipating that something like this could happen again, Enron positioned itself to exploit the opportunity if and when it came. Its downside risk was the cost of the plants—its option price—but the upside potential was enormous over a period of years. The volatility of prices was clearly the key element here.

Real options are also useful in strategic acquisitions. Martha Amram and Nalin Kulatilaka, in their book, *Real Options,* give the example of a high-tech company that wanted to invest in a smaller firm, with a view to buying a controlling interest in it if all went well. They negotiated a price of $33.2 million for a 51 percent stake two years hence; at that moment, 51 percent was worth $30.6 million. The question to be decided was the amount they had to invest *now.* The standard formula came up with a figure of $8.4 million. That was their option price—hardly a trifling sum, but much cheaper, if the target company's prospects faded, than having to come up with $30.6 million immediately.

Real option theory is exceedingly helpful in the oil and gas and other extractive industries because much of the market capitalization of these companies is represented by the developed and undeveloped reserves they own below ground. The value of the reserves fluctuates with the price these commodities fetch on the world market. In an astute article, "How To Use EVA in the Oil and Gas Industry," which appeared in the Fall 1998 issue of the *Journal of Applied Corporate Finance,* Stern Stewart's John L. McCormack and Jawanth Vytheeswaran noted that the standard EVA calculation (NOPAT less a capital charge) "could explain only about 8% of the fluctuations in shareholder wealth" of the 25 large oil and gas companies that the authors studied. (Accounting earnings could explain only 2 percent to 4 percent.) The problem is that the standard EVA measurement starts with operating profits (before making various adjustments to reflect economic reality, as we explained in Chapter 2), but the market is much more concerned with the wealth below ground. When a company makes a big strike, its stock price soars. Later, when the oil and gas are produced and marketed, the stock is likely to decline, barring any further discoveries.

As McCormack and Vytheeswaran point out:

"New discoveries are discontinuous and inherently unpredictable. Past success is not a guarantee of future success . . . . Unlike many other industries in which a successful track record in building brands and building franchises is deemed to be repeatable and sustained, the oil and gas industry appears to be much more like a straight gamble."

One qualification must be made. The unsuitability of the standard EVA measurement applies only to what the industry calls a company's "upstream" operations—exploration and production (E&P); its "downstream" operations—refining and marketing—represent no problem for standard EVA. Most of the big companies are vertically integrated, but some are only E&P companies.

McCormack and Vytheeswaran suggest several changes in EVA measurement for E&P operations. The first is to alter the method most companies use in handling their exploratory drilling costs, which usually involve more dry holes than winners. They expense the costs in the year incurred. This has the positive effect of minimizing taxes, but it also depresses earnings and gives a false picture of what's going on. In later years, profits will increase and will be given an even greater boost to the extent that managers slow down exploration. Thus, managers have a perverse incentive to stunt activity that, in the long run, increases shareholder wealth. The article's authors have no objection to expensing exploration costs for tax purposes, but propose that, in internal accounting, the exploratory costs should be capitalized. It is the same logic that in the EVA calculation mandates the capitalization of R&D and brand advertising, as well as training and development outlays incurred by financial service companies, such as banks and insurance companies.

The most important reform involves "forward-looking EVA." This is a drastic change from standard EVA measurement. Each year, McCormack and Vytheeswaran would add the enhanced value of a company's reserves—or its diminution, if prices declined—to the company's NOPAT. More specifically, as the same authors wrote, in an article in the April 1999 issue of *Oil and Gas Investor:*

> "Value creation in a specific period would be calculated by subtracting the present value of reserves at the beginning of the period from both the present value of reserves at the end of the period and of the net capital invested in reserves during that period. For example, the EVA calculation for a particular year, say 1998, would include the following adjustment:
>
> $$[\text{PV Reserves 1998} - \text{PV Reserves 1997}]$$
> $$- [\text{Net Capitalized Costs 1998}$$
> $$- \text{Net Capitalized Costs 1997}]$$
>
> Essentially, this adjustment recognizes that the market gives credit now for value to be delivered in the future."

For that reason, future prices, readily available in the financial press, are used in the calculation—not spot prices. But the exercise does not end here. The value of reserves in the year concerned is added to the firm's capital account, thereby increasing the capital charge to be deducted from the following year's NOPAT and raising the hurdle to be vaulted to continue the improvement in EVA.

To get an accurate reflection of the increase in shareholder wealth, NOPAT is also increased, year by year, by the value of the company's options. These options are of two sorts: proven but undeveloped reserves (PUDs), and probable and potential reserves. The latter are highly "iffy" and involve very complex calculations. The net present value (NPV) of proven but undeveloped reserves is easier to understand by relatively simple real-option theory. The cost of an option consists of the expense of geological and geophysical studies and the cost of leasing the land. The option's exercise price— the cost of drilling after the decision to develop is made—can be easily calculated by any firm in the business. The net present value of future cash flows (similar to the stock price in financial options) is obviously dependent on what prices will be when the wells are drilled; for the calculation, presently available future prices are used.

Finally, the economic value of all the proven but undeveloped reserves consists of the static discounted cash flow value of all the wells—the NPV if development of all of them went forward today— plus the volatility value coming from the opportunity to wait and gather more information about price changes.

In the *Journal of Applied Corporate Finance,* the authors point out:

> "Like a stock option, an undeveloped reserve will be valuable even if developing it represents a zero or negative NPV project at the present time. It will be valuable just on the chance that it will be a positive NPV project down the road [if prices rise]."

They add:

> "Once a company exercises the right to develop a reserve, the underlying asset becomes a series of linked, and usually declining, cash flows derived from producing and selling oil over many years."

But this has its advantages:

> "The cash flows generated from oil development projects tend to be significantly more volatile than crude oil futures price curves because of operational leverage. If the price of oil rises, revenues will

tend to rise faster than the costs because most of the costs are fixed and do not vary with the cost of oil. As a result, profits, cash flows and the present value of future cash flows will all rise faster than oil prices. Thus, although many oil executives lament it, the uncertainty in the price of oil, coupled with high operational leverage, is ironically what gives the options to develop undeveloped reserves much of their present value."

Forward-looking EVA for the extractive industries has two major purposes. The first is to create a measurement system that is in accord with market reality. The market responds exuberantly to news of large oil and gas discoveries; it translates the sudden increase in wealth into an upsurging share price. In their study of 25 large oil and gas companies, based only on publicly disclosed reserve values, McCormack and Vytheeswaran found that forward EVA calculations explained 49 percent of the change in shareholder wealth, whereas standard EVA, as already mentioned, explained only 8 percent. With a more sophisticated measure of reserves, forward EVA explained 66 percent of shareholder wealth. Moreover, with internal company data, the figure in some companies has gone as high as 90 percent.

The second purpose of the change is to provide a realistic incentive system. Under the standard EVA measures, oil company managers who greatly enriched their shareholders would be meagerly compensated; the increase in EVA would derive only from the increase in earnings, not from the enlargement of the company's capital base. It would be as unfair as rewarding the manager of a mutual fund for the dividend yield on investments, with nothing added for capital appreciation or total returns. Under the new dispensation, the mechanics of the standard EVA incentive program are the same: annual expected improvements, targets set in advance for three- or five-year periods, a bonus bank, no cap on bonuses. The difference is that annual increases in capital because of mineral strikes would be included in NOPAT and thus could greatly boost managerial rewards. The new system is already in place at Nuevo Energy, based in Houston, and in the oil and gas unit of Montana Power.

There is one conceivable problem with the new bonus potential in forward-looking EVA: excessive rewards resulting from enormous rises in the price of oil, such as occurred because of OPEC's action in 1973 and after the overthrow of the Shah of Iran in 1979—or the reverse, with the drastic decline in the price of oil in the mid-1980s. One of the duties of top management, of course, is to hedge against price risk, but such enormous increases or declines in price have the quality of acts of God and might be regarded as beyond the ameliorative talents of mere mortals. Thus, employment of forward-looking EVA inevitably raises fundamental questions about the quality of corporations' risk management. Companies must face not only the issue of whether to hedge commodity prices but by whose authority within the corporation. It should be the responsibility of the highest levels.

Forward-looking EVA need not be limited to extractive industries but could conceivably be applied in other fields that are subject to sudden, discontinuous increases in capital value. The pharmaceutical industry is frequently mentioned. It is similar to oil and gas in that companies are continually "prospecting"—seeking to discover new and improved drugs in the knowledge that every hit will bring a cascade of dollars during the 17-year period of patent protection. Every major drug company is pursuing a multiplicity of options: starting with initial R&D; pursuing further development if the lab results are favorable; animal testing, which, if successful, is followed by human trials; and finally, application to the FDA for approval. The option process means that, at every stage, management can cut its losses without betting the shop, and this leeway allows it to pursue a variety of opportunities at the same time. Both the bundle of options and the huge increase in capital value when a Merck, a Searle, or a Pfizer brings a major new drug to market suggest that forward-looking EVA would be the appropriate measure.

Real option theory also tends to explain the huge capitalizations of Internet companies that have yet to show any accounting earnings. Michael J. Mauboussin, of Crédit Suisse First Boston, in a research paper released in June 1999, argues that many high-flying stocks are not overpriced, as many market analysts believe. In his view, the analysts err because they rely exclusively on discounted cash flow analysis and ignore "the potentially meaningful value of imbedded real options." He then suggests that "stocks of companies that participate in highly uncertain markets are best viewed as a combination of the discounted cash flow value of the current known businesses plus a portfolio of real options." Then comes a big leap: [the value of the options] "can be estimated by taking the difference between the current equity value and the DCF value of the established businesses." This formulation suggests that speculative frenzy or fantasy plays no role whatsoever in these soaring stock prices, though he goes on to say that "reasonable people may disagree about the value of the imbedded real options."

Mauboussin's main point, however, is valid: the hidden options have real value. He later analyzes Amazon.com, calling it "an options smorgasbord." In summary:

"The company started by selling books. So there was a DCF value for the book business, plus out-of-the-money contingent options on other offerings. As the book business proved successful, the contingent option on music went from out-of-the-money to in-the-money, spurring the music investment. As the music business thrived, the company exercised an option to get into videos. As time has passed, Amazon's real options portfolio has become more valuable. For example, the recent foray into the auction business, unimaginable one year ago, was contingent on a large base of qualified users. Many analysts assert that a business like Amazon cannot be realistically valued. We disagree. The key is attributing explicit value to the company's real options. And that value is potentially huge."

One need not share the exuberance of the true believers to concede the main point: real options are valuable tools.

Chapter 12

25 Questions

Over the years, at hundreds of EVA presentations and one-on-one sessions with CEOs and CFOs, Joel Stern has been confronted with a variety of questions about both the theoretical fundaments of EVA and its practical applications. We thought it might be helpful to respond to several of the most frequently asked questions, even at the risk of repeating some material previously dealt with.

Some of the questions have been simple and straightforward; others have been much more complex, deriving from both the theories of modern finance—valuation, portfolio, options pricing, and agency—and, more specifically, from a subset of these theories, Economic Value Added. They deal with the determinants of value, risk management, the evaluation of new investment opportunities, and the overarching theme of how more perfectly to align the interests of both managers and employees with those of the shareholders.

In microeconomic theory, the prevailing view, to which we fervently adhere, is that maximizing shareholder value simultaneously maximizes the wealth of society, including such stakeholders as labor, suppliers, customers, and the community at large. There is no

conflict between the interests of shareholders and other stakeholders, but the latter cannot benefit unless the shareholders—the
providers of capital—get their due. If the shareholders are scanted
over a period of time, the corporation's viability is threatened, to
everybody's detriment.

Question 1. *Why are companies in the private sector, as well as state-
owned enterprises, turning to economic profit as a measure of performance, and what has been the catalyst?*

A. The answer can be crisply stated: profits calculated by standard accounting methods often distort the economic reality of the
firm, as we argued at length in Chapter 1. Economic profit, the
generic term for EVA, provides a far truer picture of what is going
on. To be sure, there was a time, decades ago, when the relationship between the accounting concept of net income—the so-
called bottom line—served as a reasonable guide to measuring
performance. Its correlation with changes in share value was fairly
high. The way to measure the association was to look at movements in share values and movements in the bottom line over the
business cycle. Put another way, for publicly traded firms on stock
exchanges, the question was: "Was the price-to-earnings ratio reasonably stable over the business cycle?" More often than not, the
answer was "Yes."

Unfortunately, Generally Accepted Accounting Principles
(GAAP) suffered many alterations that caused the relationship
between share values and net income to become less closely associated. For example, under pooling accounting for acquisitions,
firms that exchanged common stock were able to report the merger
without specifying the premium paid by the buyer. In short, all of
the accounts of both companies were merely consolidated and,
thus, no premium was shown. If the acquisition was made by cash

or senior securities, however, so-called purchase accounting had to be used. The buyer had to record the premium paid—the excess of the purchase price over the fair value of the company bought— and this premium, oddly called "good will," had to be written off as an expense against earnings during a period not to exceed 40 years. The annual charge reduced net income and earnings per share and, for managers who received incentives tied to the bottom line, was clearly inferior to pooling. Of course, the economics of the transaction were fundamentally the same. Pooling has enjoyed an enormous popularity for many years, despite the veil of unreality it cast over transactions—or rather, because of it—one of the many ironies caused by accounting rules.

A second aberration has been the arbitrary expensing of large capital expenditures by high-technology firms for research and development. Until 1975, R&D was capitalized on the balance sheet as an asset and then amortized against bottom-line profits over varying periods of time, depending on the expected useful life of the R&D. Firms selected different periods for the life of R&D, depending on their varying estimates of its future impact. But the accounting profession's ruling body, having decided that comparability was much more important, adopted the most conservative alternative: expensing R&D in the year in which it was paid for. This approach assumes that the return on R&D is so uncertain that it is limited to the current year. The result is that high-technology firms' profitability is grievously understated, as are their assets and shareholder equity. This is due, of course, to these firms' high volume of R&D spending, and thus there is no way realistically to compare their profitability with that of ordinary manufacturing firms. The uniformity imposed to make comparisons easier has distorted economic reality. And there are many other examples, as detailed in Chapter 1. Hence the desire, on the part of many firms, to measure economic profit as opposed to accounting profit.

Question 2. *What determines how broadly and how deeply EVA is deployed in an organization?*

A. The extent to which the EVA measurement penetrates an organization is a function of three things. The first is the commitment of the chief executive to getting the measure right—not just at the top of the organization, based on consolidated results, but right down through the organization, even to the shop floor. A second factor that determines the depth of the measurement system is the degree to which incentives have accompanied it. Thus, as incentives based on economic profit are carried down through middle management, one can be reasonably certain that economic profit will be measured at least that far down in the organization.

The third factor is the degree to which measurement of economic profit makes sense at various levels of the organization. One problem that needs to be resolved is determining transfer prices between various parts of the firm. A related issue is shared resources, which requires reasonably accurate allocation of net assets between units. There is a fourth factor that can become important: early consultation with unions to win their support. There is no reason why unionized hourly workers cannot participate in an incentive compensation process based on EVA. Union workers at Briggs & Stratton and at Tower Automotive, for example, are covered by EVA and, as discussed in Chapter 6, a growing movement for union–management cooperation in Europe provides an environment conducive to the adoption of EVA on the shop floor.

Question 3. *Does the type of remuneration drive investment decisions?*

A. The answer is that these two issues, although not usually related in normal conversations in the boardroom, or among executive committees of firms, are in fact integrally connected. If compensation is related to something other than EVA improvement—especially the variable pay component of compensation—then we would expect that management behavior would further whatever course of action the incentive system promotes.

For example, let us assume that managers' remuneration was tied to improvement in net profit after taxes—or its derivative, earnings per share—rather than increases in EVA. Managers might then be expected to cut back on new worthwhile investments that have positive net present values, if investing in such projects would lead to short-term declines in profitability, as a result of start-up costs, learning costs, and training and development costs, all of which are expensed in the current year against profitability. One can imagine many other examples of the perverse effects of the wrong incentives.

Question 4. *How is the task of investor relations altered by employing an EVA framework?*

A. Historically, the attitude of most senior managements has been to release information on a need-to-know basis, subject to the legal principle of not misleading investors by providing them with unrealistic expectations of the future, but rather focusing on historic information that can be documented. Thus, annual reports and quarterly financial statements typically present historical information with very general and usually noncommittal statements about a company's future performance.

In contrast, investors need to make their own judgments about expected future performance. Virtually all serious finance, accounting, and strategy scholars at major business schools believe that the current value of a firm is based on its expected future performance. The only relevance of historical information for the pricing of shares is the extent to which historical information is useful in forming expectations about the future. The reason the EVA framework is so important to investment analysts who attempt to determine intrinsic value is that they have great difficulty in assessing the likelihood that managers will behave in the interest of shareholders. We all know that managers' direct remuneration is largely tied to the size of the firm and the magnitude of their responsibilities. Thus, the growth of the firm is often a sufficient condition for management's success. Shareholders require much more—namely, that the company earn at least the required rate of return for the risk involved.

When management announces that a full EVA implementation will occur, management is, in effect, communicating to the market that projects that could be expected to earn inadequate rates of return are likely to be rejected, and growth for its own sake will also be rejected. This provides investment analysts with greater confidence about the future course of a company's performance. It is also the reason why almost all firms that implement EVA include their EVA performance in their annual reports, in quarterly statements, and especially in presentations to societies of investment analysts. There is no question that those managements that are willing to talk about EVA in public are making a special statement to the world of investors.

Question 5. *Feedback from many of your clients is that the effort required to introduce EVA is underestimated and insufficiently stressed. Your comments?*

A. It is true that the initial work that is involved in implementing an EVA program can appear to be simple, straightforward, and limited in senior management's commitment, but, in reality, two major efforts should occur simultaneously if the program is to be successful.

First, a steering committee should be set up, consisting of the firm's executive or management committee, including all senior operating management, as well as the chief executive officer, the chief financial officer, the chief operating officer, and the head of human resources. The purpose of the steering committee, which should meet about once a month, is to make major policy decisions on the design and structure of the EVA program. The committee responds to more than 150 questions that come from Stern Stewart & Co. They include issues of measurement, such as adjustments to accounting income and capital to eliminate the anomalies we have previously discussed, as well as a management system that essentially rewrites the capital budgeting system for the evaluation of new investment opportunities, including mergers and acquisitions.

If designed properly, the EVA management system should also serve to evaluate all existing activities, so that, in effect, the firm is engaged in zero-based budgeting, examining all aspects of the firm to see where value is being created and where it is being destroyed—not just for new investments, but also for existing activities.

The steering committee is also concerned with the design of the incentive compensation system. The committee has to decide such crucial elements as the payout period, the type of bonus bank to be used, and whether some part of the bonus should be in the form of shares or share options or whether it should all be cash.

The second major part of an EVA implementation involves changing the mind-set of the organization through a carefully designed orientation and training program. Training is mostly the responsibility of the head of human resources, with support from the financial office. There should be a formal implementation team with representatives also from finance and accounting, planning, and operations. The implementation team reports directly to the steering committee.

Implementing an EVA program is not something that occurs only over a period of a few months. Rather, it involves an abiding commitment of the corporate culture to a measurement/management/incentive system that requires all employees to understand the important role that they can play in enhancing EVA and, thus, shareholder value.

Question 6. *Most EVA companies have adopted additional criteria for bonus evaluation. Your comments?*

A. There is no question that EVA need not be the only measure used in developing a bonus system. Clearly, personal goals and strategic objectives can also be included. But it is equally apparent that companies should not reward employees for achieving such goals if they also do not deliver EVA improvement. Put another way: the funding of a bonus system should come from the improvement in EVA. Bonuses for achieving other goals should be paid only if EVA improvement occurs. If this were not the case, individuals would be tempted to bypass the central goal of EVA gains by arguing that they were otherwise successful. Their formulation might be: "I may not have delivered on EVA, but I sure have achieved my strategic and personal goals, and look how happy our customers and suppliers are." The problem with this argument, of course, is that it justifies rewarding employees for nonquantifiable achievements, while penalizing shareholders because of the shortfall in EVA.

Question 7. *The first year of EVA is critical in getting buy-in on the bonus plan. What is your experience in balancing the effect on EPS and paying the bonus?*

A. Putting in a new bonus plan is difficult because people have learned how to live in the existing environment. Thus, it is always a good idea to have a strong result in the first year of the EVA program. However, to say that EVA should be balanced in some manner with improvements in earnings per share misses the point of EVA entirely. The drive to improve EPS is sometimes in conflict with the growth of EVA, as we have been at pains to point out. It is our view that the market is sophisticated about EVA improvements and that if there is a conflict between EVA and the accounting results, the EPS shortfall will not cause a negative effect on the share price. This is true as long as the firm's commitment to its EVA program is believed by the "lead steer" investors—those knowledgeable types who influence the herd of the less sophisticated.

Question 8. *One of the concerns expressed by EVA clients is dysfunctional behavior between departments when someone's EVA may be threatened by someone else's proposal. What are your experiences?*

A. This concern explains why it is so important to have dynamic discussions, in the steering committee, about ways to get people to work together in building the consolidated EVA for the company as a whole. From time to time, an ombudsman may be necessary to choose between conflicting goals, but this is not new. All firms experience conflicts between individual units—situations in which the pursuit of unit objectives, if achieved, would damage the firm as a whole. It is our view that the guiding purpose of the executive committee of any company is to be the ombudsman and to determine the appropriate choices. Firms that go on EVA do not experience any more or less of these conflicts than non-EVA firms. It is necessary that lines of communication remain open and that the design of the EVA bonus system is such that the key players at the top of the organization are motivated to focus on maximizing consolidated EVA.

Question 9. *How linked has EVA been with the development of a Balanced Scorecard—was it a help or a hindrance?*

A. The fact that EVA and the management and incentive system known as the balanced scorecard have been of interest to senior management and boards of directors is evidence that the accounting framework suffers from shortcomings in providing management not only with a way to keep score, but also with an approach that more closely aligns the interests of employees with those of shareholders. Movements in EVA track the increase and decrease in the firm's economic value—the primary concern of shareholders. By contrast, the balanced scorecard attempts to refocus management goals away from simple accounting net income and such popular earnings measures as return on equity, to a number of other critical issues that all firms face: relations with suppliers and customers, achieving primary operating objectives, and so on. There is no conflict between EVA and the balanced scorecard, as attested by Dr. Robert Kaplan of the Harvard Business School, one of the coauthors of the scorecard. In fact, he has recommended that a company adopting his approach should use EVA as the financial measure in the scorecard and tie incentives to EVA improvement.

The only problem with the balanced scorecard, as viewed by an EVA proponent, is that it tends to take senior management's eye off the key driver of shareholder value, and it might also create circumstances that would reward management for achieving other than financial objectives, so that shareholder interests would suffer. Put another way, the balanced scorecard provides valuable information for management, but it should never be the key driver of performance and rewards, especially at the expense of EVA.

Question 10. *What have been the effects of EVA on the culture and behavior of businesses?*

A. There have been several positive consequences. The easiest way to respond to this question is to consider a Rorschach test on two disparate issues in corporate strategy over the past 20 years. First, consider a Rorschach reaction to the popular slogan, "Process reengineering." The normal response is: "You're fired!" By contrast, the immediate reaction when EVA is mentioned is, "How can we build value together?" In other words, EVA is inclusive, not exclusive. One reason is that measures of performance are designed within EVA centers, which are focuses of responsibility for achieving improvements in shareholder value. This means that all employees become participants or, better still, partners in improvements in EVA, and, where management permits, are included in the incentive system as well.

That arrangement is highly desirable. Look at it this way: the senior executives in a firm might create $100 in value, whereas a shop-floor worker might create only $1 of value. The point to keep in mind, however, is that the number of people down through the organization far outnumber the senior management, and it is a shame not to solicit their contribution by making them part of the EVA thrust. Organizations that have carried EVA deep down into the ranks have tapped talent and initiative that would have otherwise remained dormant.

Question 11. *If we go for incentive remuneration, how do you measure that at, say, group level, or is it only done at company level, using EVA?*

A. Incentives work well at whatever level of responsibility is being measured. For senior management, the appropriate measure of performance is the company-wide improvement of EVA. Further down in the organization, it is best to measure EVA at each local EVA center and reward its people for the improvement in locally generated EVA. Of course, in many organizations, it is difficult to measure EVA deep down in the structure, because of the problems of shared resources and transfer pricing. The resolution of these problems often means that only a part of EVA will be measured and rewarded. Still, such a system appears to be much superior to the alternatives of either having no incentive system at all, or making it arbitrary or subject to negotiation.

Question 12. *Does EVA influence the decisions of a board of directors with respect to investing in the organic growth of a company? How do you overcome siloism/parochialism?*

A. Under the EVA banner, the optimal procedure is zero-based budgeting; all activities of the firm are reevaluated every year as if the decision to invest in them was being made all over again, in order to decide if the investment is likely to enhance value. The benefit of this approach is that all investments are treated in exactly the same manner. This means that all mergers and acquisitions, usually referred to as external growth, are examined and prioritized, on the basis of prospective EVA improvement, in exactly the same way as new investments in existing activities. Often, the latter type is called internal or organic growth.

Siloism can be a real problem. Within individual EVA centers, the clear focus of individuals on maximizing the improvement in EVA within the center can lead to a lack of concern and even an unwitting sabotage of what is happening elsewhere in the company. It is up to senior executives to overcome this parochialism by insisting on the primacy of company-wide objectives. The reward structure should be fashioned to reinforce this discipline. EVA bonuses for top unit managers are generally based in part on unit performance, and in part on consolidated results. Corporate officers are compensated on corporate results alone, as previously mentioned. In addition, unit managers often participate in stock option programs, which reinforce their stake in the success of the firm as a whole. We should also point out that the company-wide-versus-silos conflict does encourage vital internal discussions that reinforce commitments to EVA. It is a useful part of the training process.

Question 13. *In looking at EVA as an incentive tool, has it been effective? If it has not, why not?*

A. The answer is that nothing is perfect. Where EVA has not worked well as an incentive device, it has usually been because of the failure of the CEO or other members of the executive committee to really champion the program and to drill it down into the organization. We have to recognize a fact of life: senior management has been accustomed to working with other reward systems that have involved negotiations of budgets, and they have learned how to game the system. EVA presents a new challenge to such people. To senior managers who have been around for several decades, EVA can represent a threat to the stability of their lives. That is why the role of the CEO is so important in making the EVA program a success.

Question 14. *How easy is it for individuals who do not have well-developed business and financial acumen to grasp the concept of EVA and thus understand how it impacts on them, and what they can do to impact EVA?*

A. There is no simple answer to this. Admittedly, when Stern Stewart began the process of designing incentives to go with the EVA measure, the initial belief was that incentives would work almost exclusively at the senior-management level of the organization. This was especially clear in G. Bennett Stewart III's volume, *The Quest for Value.* The sixth chapter, which is devoted to the incentive story, is entitled "Making Managers into Owners." The emphasis was on management, not employees deeper in the organization.

Only after the passage of time and scores and scores of EVA implementations did Stern Stewart conclude that the program could be pushed into the lower rungs of the organization. Briggs & Stratton was among the first to recognize the approach that should be used: a crafting of nontechnical examples of financial principles that could easily be grasped by everybody.

This success was followed by many others, but it is instructive that it was government organizations that placed a requirement on Stern Stewart that all the employees must be in the program in order for it to be applicable to senior management. This was the case at the South African Institute for Medical Research (SAIMR); at Eskom, the state-owned electric utility in South Africa; and now at Telkom, the country's state-owned telecommunications organization. A particularly noteworthy example is the United States Postal Service, where the Board of Governors insisted that EVA be designed so that all employees could be measured and rewarded on the basis of EVA. The unions of nonsupervisory employees opted out, however. It is also interesting that public utilities in the United States have encouraged Stern Stewart to design EVA programs to be used throughout their organizations. These corporations are nonelitist and believe that respect for the individual at every level is crucial to the success of all.

Thus, it is no problem at all to make EVA understandable to people who have either limited formal education or limited knowledge of finance and accounting. It reminds us of the story of a student studying physics at a university. The student returns home to the family farm—and to the query, "What have you learned in physics this year?" "It's very complicated," the student replies, whereupon his father puts him down with, "So this means you don't understand it?"

Our view is that if you do understand a complex issue, you can describe it in terms that will be understandable to one and all, usually by employing everyday examples of behavioral change that the organization wants to achieve. At the end of a training session at a trucking firm in the United States, one of the participants raised his hand and said, "I don't get it. What do you want me to do differently from what I did yesterday?" To which the instructor replied, "Are you an owner-operator, or do you drive a truck owned by the company?" The latter was the case. "That's where the problem lies," the instructor said. "Nobody seems to know why it is that the company drivers only obtain 6.2 miles to the gallon when the owner-operators get 6.8. I believe a company driver at the top of a hill cannot resist the temptation to slam his foot down on the accelerator and take his rig down the hill at 90 mph. What do you do? Do you lift your foot at the top of the hill like the owner-operator? And what about your safety record? The owner-operators have a serious accident once every six or seven years, but you company drivers are much more accident-prone." The driver responded, "All right, I will lift my foot at the top of the hill and I will be as safe as the owner-operators. Does that mean that I will receive a bonus declaration next year, equal to that of the owner-operators?"

Question 15. *What is the best approach to use in the education process?*

A. Much depends on the degree to which an organization appears willing to make fundamental changes in the corporate culture. In relatively young, fast-moving, progressive companies, a couple of training sessions may be all that is necessary for the bulk of employees, though more extensive sessions are needed for the leaders. (This is described in Chapter 7.) In companies with an inbred, sluggish management structure that is historically resistant to change, and an aging workforce, more extensive training is necessary, along with a more gradual approach.

Under these circumstances, it is best to have the training and development process comprise three distinct sessions for the bulk of the employees. Each session should last only 45 minutes and be followed by an extensive question-and-answer session. The first session is entitled "What Is EVA and Why Are We Doing It Now?" The purpose of this session is merely to introduce the fundamental ideas of economic value, to define EVA, and to explain why the current tide requires an alteration in the performance measurement and management system of the company. Usually, it is a good idea to include a brief history of the change in the competitive environment, including globalization. The objective here is to make certain that all employees realize that times have changed, and one of the important responses is to adopt a focus on shareholder value.

The second session is devoted to measuring EVA—both at the consolidated level of the firm and at the different EVA centers in which the employees work. In addition, the forward plans of the EVA centers are set forth and are examined to determine whether they are EVA positive, zero, or negative.

The third session is devoted entirely to the incentive compensation system, assuming it is carried down to the specific EVA center. The session also presents specifics of the way EVA is used by management to evaluate investment opportunities.

Question 16. *In what type of organization (referring to culture, way of working) does EVA succeed best, and why?*

A. Unfortunately, EVA succeeds best where a major crisis has called into question the business practices and fundamental behavior of the organization—in short, a situation in which the word "change" shouts out at all employees and says "Now!" Often, the chief executive has also been replaced, and the new arrival wants abrupt alterations in behavior and performance.

At Briggs & Stratton, it was a crisis in performance, resulting in the company losing money for the first time in decades. At SPX, a new CEO arrived from General Electric and wanted abrupt improvements and a complete makeover of attitudes on the part of employees. At Herman Miller, a firm already accustomed to focus on productivity and employee participation, the crisis was caused by a hemorrhage of capital and by administrative chaos in the planning process, all of which led to a new CEO and CFO.

True, these are extreme cases. Less severe is the change to globalization and the "new economy," which requires managers to become more critical and responsive to shareholder value, productivity gains, investment opportunities, and ways to make human capital more productive.

Question 17. *What formulas are used in the calculation of EVA-based incentive programs? Are there many variations that have been adopted? Which works best?*

A. At the consolidated level of the firm, as mentioned in the response to Question 11, the EVA of the firm is used, and the incentives are tied to EVA improvements. As noted earlier, we recommend that EVA be used as a funding source for all incentive payments, but that nonquantifiable criteria—the personal and strategic goals—be considered simultaneously, to represent no more than 25 percent of the total reward.

As EVA is drilled down deeper into the organization, below the level of the executive committee, it is best to calculate EVA improvements for the individual units of the firm, where the boundaries of function and accountability are sufficiently clear to make EVA measurement practical. The lines of demarcation vary, of course, from company to company. It can be a division, a business unit, a factory. As mentioned earlier, to avoid siloism, the head of the unit (and perhaps his or her deputy) receives bonuses based in part (25 percent or more) on corporate EVA and the rest on unit EVA. Personnel below that rank are totally incentivized on unit EVA, for that is the only arena that they can affect.

There are two basic types of EVA incentive programs. The first, often called the "all-in" bank, takes the entire declaration of the EVA bonus and deposits it into a bonus bank. A fraction of it is then paid out in the current period as an award. The remainder is held at risk and is subject to loss if the improvement in EVA for which the bonus was awarded is not sustained. The normal payout period runs about six years, and 70 percent is disbursed in the first three years.

The second type, involving the "threshold bank," pays out the full amount of the bonus for the year earned. If the EVA performance exceeds the year's target, the additional bonus is sequestered in the bonus bank and is distributed over a three-year period. Although this second approach has become the more popular one in the United States, it has the disadvantage of placing less money at risk in the bonus bank. Thus, it does not provide as lengthy a time horizon for the individual participant as does the "all-in" bonus bank. In Europe, South Africa, and Australia, the latter type is predominant because boards of directors prefer to use a large at-risk component to motivate intermediate and long-term behavior. There are a variety of reasons for wishing to use one or the other type of bonus bank, depending on the culture of the organization and the history and preferences of the executive committee with incentive systems.

One final comment: the target amounts of EVA performance necessary for regular and excess bonus can be larger or smaller, depending on the risk preference of top management. In our opinion, one must be very careful in designing incentives, to make certain that participants in the program understand how much they can gain or lose for every dollar of improvement or deterioration in EVA. For example, public utilities and state-owned enterprises have traditionally favored relatively low risk in the compensation structure. We recommend that the risk profile in the design of the EVA system be more moderate than in other industries. In organizations that are at the other extreme of the risk spectrum, such as high-technology firms, one must be careful not to build an EVA system that is excessively risky. The business itself is very risky, and risk on top of risk could lead to a "bet the farm" attitude, which clearly would be undesirable for the shareholders.

Question 18. *What kind of continuing relationship is desirable between the client company and the outside consultant?*

A. Clients should insist on the transfer of the template and the working papers of the consulting organization, as part of the knowledge transfer. This is actually a transfer of technology from the consulting organization to the client. For this reason alone, the consulting organization will likely insist that no transfer of the technology beyond the client is permissible.

As part of the implementation, the client should insist on regular meetings as often as four times a year for the first few years after the implementation, to make certain that questions arising from the program are quickly answered, and conflicts are resolved. No system can be expected to work perfectly from the outset.

Question 19. *What is a good time frame for implementation of this system?*

A. The length of time needed for a successful implementation for senior management and their immediate direct reports is between eight months and one year, if the firm is in only a few business categories. The greater the number of people in the firm and the greater the complexity and size of the organization, the longer it takes to implement the program. At Siemens, in Germany, which has 17 different businesses, the time frame ran to more than 17 months. In organizations that have carried the program down to middle management and then drilled it down virtually to the shop floor, the first part of the program absorbed between 15 and 18 months, and the second part added another year to 18 months.

In government organizations, which are more alien to the concept of economic profit than are private companies, a great deal more care is taken at each stage of the implementation. As a consequence, the time frames lengthen. The first part of the program for senior management runs about a year to 18 months, and there is a long extension when the program is carried down to the shop floor. A great deal of time and effort is needed to build consensus and to demonstrate natural outcomes through simulations.

Question 20. *What is the minimum financial system that a client must have in order to implement EVA successfully?*

A. The firm needs information that would normally be found on income statements and balance sheets down through an organization. Many firms do not report this way internally; for them, the minimal requirements are: a profit and loss statement, and the items on a balance sheet that the individual units' managers need to run their businesses. It is not easy to generalize on this particular subject, because staff support centers and cost centers do not have much in the form of balance sheet information. Keep in mind that we are seeking the information that is necessary to measure the controllable aspect of EVA or EVA drivers.

Question 21. *How do you devise EVA indicators for service departments?*

A. Service departments—finance, planning, legal, and human resources, to mention only the most obvious ones—should have their results measured by the consolidated results of the organization they serve. For example, the chief financial officer and staff serving the consolidated firm should be measured by the results of the latter, whereas a divisional or subsidiary controller should be measured by the results of that unit.

Service departments, however, might also want to utilize soft, subjective measures that deal with customer satisfaction—in this case, the specific operating units that they serve, or other personal and strategic objectives that are deemed to be very important. These soft issues should represent a larger percentage of total variable compensation than is received by the typical operating person. Where the operating people typically have as much as 25 percent of variable pay determined by strategic and personal objectives, service organizations might have as much as 50 percent. These employees are subject to review by the organization that they serve, and the review determines a good part of the subjective pay. "360" reviews (I review him, and he reviews me) are exceptionally useful devices for gathering valuable information in human resources management, and we have recommended them as a course of action in numerous EVA implementations, but only where the corporate culture was ready for such a suggestion.

Question 22. *If you have a whole range of organizational initiatives and priorities, which may be in conflict with short- or long-term financial goals, how do you deal with this? You need something to ensure that the business units can drive EVA, but only after meeting personnel, societal, and customer goals and targets.*

A. It is often stipulated that a number of organizational initiatives and priorities could be in conflict with improvements in EVA, over either the very short or the intermediate term. In our view, such initiatives usually contribute to improvement in EVA. Where they don't, they should be carefully evaluated to see whether such initiatives are actually worthwhile. For example, when customer satisfaction is incorporated into an EVA culture, we have difficulty understanding how it conflicts with EVA improvement.

Consider the matter of safety in the workplace. Expenditures to promote safety may appear to some as a worthless investment that will lower EVA, but obviously such a view is extremely shortsighted. Mining companies that have implemented EVA have used safety in the mine as a highly desirable soft issue that is part of the variable pay component. One company announced it would cancel bonus declarations entirely if the safety tolerance fell short of the desired level. In the case of rural electrification in South Africa, we recommended that safety goals be regarded as societal in nature, and once the capital has been allocated to achieve them, it should be excluded from the EVA bonus calculation. Such investments are then neutralized, which means that they have no bearing on EVA improvement going forward.

Question 23. *How do you best determine whether EVA results are derived from internal efforts rather than market impacts?*

A. An impact on EVA, whether it is derived from discretionary managerial decisions or just plain good luck from exogenous forces, should have no bearing on the EVA program. Occasionally, good luck or bad luck affects company outcomes, and the EVA rewards are not simply the result of managerial wisdom. This is not a bad thing; if good luck boosts profits or the share price, and thus rewards the shareholders, then good luck should also reward employees. Bad luck affects everybody in the same fashion, but the bonus bank plays a mitigating role for employees. If the company suffers reversals through bad luck, employees still get a payout from the bonus bank, drawn from the money sequestered during the good years.

Question 24. *Change caused by EVA is said to be radical. Describe what may happen.*

A. Whether the change wrought by EVA is radical depends on the existing corporate culture. In firms where the corporate objective has been size-for-its-own-sake (expressed as market share, for example), EVA can represent radical change. On the other hand, in companies run in close alignment with shareholder interests, the change to EVA merely provides a highly objective means for calculating increases in value. Here the company is engaged in relatively minor adjustments—it is attempting to reach a set of world class/best practices. For this type of firm, the EVA story is the answer to the question: "How high is high, and how much can we really achieve?"

In many organizations that implement EVA, the company is in turmoil and a new chief executive is trying to turn things around; or, the company is suffering from exogenous factors that have caused morale to weaken dramatically; or, perhaps the regulatory structure is changing quickly from one of regulation to deregulation. In all these situations, management systems and practices require huge alterations and improvements. Whatever the story, it is interesting to note that, in firms that incorporate the Stern Stewart bonus architecture, typically there is a huge alteration in the market's perception of the quality of management and its strategic plans. Here is a quick review of the bonus architecture:

1. Use EVA and only EVA to determine the major part of the bonus (apart from the "soft goals"). Use of other measures dilutes focus.
2. Set definitive, multiyear targets. This guarantees continuing significant rewards for sustained, strong performance, and it prevents sacrificing the future for short-term gains.
3. Derive targets from investors' expectations. Combined with multiyear targets, this prevents "gaming" the plan. Executives are free to develop stretch goals and drive for their achievement. Minimal time is wasted on budget negotiations.
4. Avoid caps and floors. This prevents the "go golfing" mentality of holding back in outstanding years, and the tendency to turn weak years into terrible ones if threshold bonus amounts will not be earned.

5. Provide bonus bank deferrals. These protect shareholders and contribute to the retention of successful management teams.

Question 25. *Timing—top-down approach first, or full rollout to all business units?*

A. This is solely a function of the chief executive's objective in implementing EVA. Most firms prefer to proceed layer by layer, beginning with the executive committee members and their immediate direct reports. The goal in year one should be no less than that, but most organizations attempt to carry it down to middle management in the first year. Extending EVA further down into the organization is the effort for year two and beyond, because education, training, and development are all crucial to willing acceptance. Companies are not democracies, but EVA works best when all people want to be players.

Chapter 13

Recipe for Success

The subtitle of this book is "Implementing Valued-Added Change in an Organization." It seems appropriate to conclude by listing six key factors that promise success, however schematic or simplistic such enumeration may seem after the carefully qualified responses to the questions in the previous chapter. Here is our short list:

1. The company must have a viable business strategy and appropriate organizational architecture before EVA can boost performance, as we have argued at length. EVA cannot rescue a company with a misconceived strategy or with products that have little potential market appeal; a company must have a *raison d'être*, apart from a desire to make money. Strategy and structure normally precede full EVA implementation, though EVA calculations can be useful in weighing alternatives.

2. To achieve the full potential of EVA, a company should install all of EVA's components—a measurement system, a management system, and an incentive system. Simply measuring EVA without using it to guide managerial decisions amounts to little more than an academic exercise. Few companies actually limit themselves to that degree, but they may not act on EVA calculations in all areas of capital outlays—acquisitions, divestitures, new products, plant expansion or contraction, and so on. Such corporate considerations as growth for its own sake, prestige, and loyalty to historic brands may override rigorous EVA calculations. EVA can hardly flourish under such circumstances.

3. An EVA incentive plan is essential, and it should reach as far down in the organization as possible. There is no more powerful prod to action than monetary reward, despite the refusal of many Europeans to acknowledge that fact of life. The best incentive plans are uncapped; limiting rewards inevitably limits potential exertion and thus potential achievements. Plans should also include deferred payout schemes with their attendant risks, to ensure that management does not sacrifice the future for present gains. As we discussed in Chapter 9, the "all-in" bank is the best type. It puts more money at risk than the threshold bank, if future performance falls off.

As a practical matter, some companies are not in a position to install an EVA incentive plan when they adopt EVA. As already mentioned, The Manitowoc Company successfully used EVA as a measurement tool to gain control over capital outlays before installing an EVA incentive plan. The initiative worked as a temporary measure, because of the CEO's firm control. The point is: it was just a temporary expedient, not a permanent arrangement.

Other companies, because of internal pressures, have had to compromise on the design of their incentive plans. One large Stern Stewart client, headquartered in the eastern region of the United States, has an incentive plan based one-third on EVA and two-thirds on operating income (two-thirds on EPS for corporate headquarters). At the risk of being called purists, we have to say that this scheme pulls in different directions. Operating income and EPS growth can come by squandering capital; EVA imposes capital discipline. Which incentive wins out? Stern Stewart advised against such a plan but the company's management was unwilling to impose an entirely new incentive scheme on its divisional executives; it argued as well that EVA would force controls on unnecessary capital expenditures that might otherwise be undertaken to boost operating income. Gradually, the company is likely to increase the percentage of bonus based on EVA.

4. A comprehensive training program is equally essential. It should not be limited to top executives but should infiltrate all managerial levels and, ideally, reach down to the shop floor. The training program of Bestfoods, a multinational company with $9 billion in sales in 63 countries, can stand as a model. First, the company trained 150 EVA experts in corporate and divisional headquarters in the United States, Europe, and Latin America. These were individuals not necessarily in the upper echelons who were given intensive training over a four-day period, and they came away with technical knowledge that allowed them to become in-house resources for anyone in the organization who was hung up on an EVA problem. They could do the detailed analyses and make the calculations. (Briggs & Stratton calls these people "internal EVA consultants").

Thereafter, Bestfoods exposed 1,000 of its senior managers to two-day training sessions; these key decision makers were expected to incorporate EVA analyses into their day-to-day work. A four-person Stern Stewart team conducted some 40 classes (25 attendees per class), inculcating the concepts through case studies over a two-day period. Classes were held in Englewood Cliffs, New Jersey, where Bestfoods has its headquarters, as well as in Chicago, Los Angeles, Toronto, Latin America, England, Belgium, Italy, Thailand, the Philippines, and China. It was one of the most extensive training programs that Stern Stewart has ever undertaken.

5. The EVA program must have the full and fervent backing of the CEO, who should chair the all-important steering committee that puts EVA in place. The CEO must not only identify value creation as the mission of the company, but must seize every opportunity—the annual sales meeting, a monthly operations review, or the annual shareholders' meeting—to preach the benefits of EVA.

In our experience, some CEOs with nonfinancial backgrounds—for example, in sales, operations, or engineering—may be reluctant to commit to a program that they perceive to be driven by a "financial" measure. EVA should be thought of as an economic as opposed to a financial or accounting measure, and the best value practitioners are those who manage to "unlearn" whatever training they might have received in the more arcane principles of financial accounting. In many ways, the use of economic profit as a performance measure is far more intuitive than any measure based on accounting earnings.

Almost without exception, wherever you find a successful EVA implementation, you will find a chief executive dedicated to the program. That is true of John McGrath of Diageo, John Blystone of SPX, Mike Volkema of Herman Miller, David Sussman of the J.D. Group in South Africa, Roderick Deane of Telecom New Zealand, Waldemar Schmidt of International Service Systems, and the CEO of just about every company whose success with EVA we have mentioned. At Briggs & Stratton, CEO Fred Stratton fortifies the EVA message at every opportunity. Quarterly board meetings include EVA progress reports, and the expected profitability of major corporate initiatives proposed to the board is evaluated, using EVA projections. Quarterly meetings with all salaried employees include corporate as well as divisional EVA performance reports. And EVA proves useful in dealing with the investment community as well, for security analysts closely track EVA in evaluating a company's future prospects.

6. The CFO and/or the controller should be equally committed. Because they have to deal simultaneously with standard accounting practices, these specialists may have an even greater problem focusing on value creation than a CEO newly introduced to EVA. Compliance with the detailed reporting requirements of the SEC and the market is a large part of their job. When they are immersed in these logic-defying principles of financial accounting, many of them are challenged to develop and support a sensible, broadly understandable system for measuring economic value.

Thus, the most valuable CFOs are those who have developed an in-depth understanding of the key principles of EVA. These are professionals who can walk through a factory and tell whether the operating assets are being deployed efficiently, and who have a sixth sense about whether a proposed merger will offer sufficient integrating efficiencies to justify the merger premium, transaction costs, and any possible costs stemming from the loss of managerial independence and incentive. Effective CFOs can also add value by moving the firm closer to the optimal capital structure, by working with the human resources specialists in developing appropriate compensation programs, and by helping the operating, technical, and marketing people to motivate behavior that creates value in their divisions and departments.

None of this is easy, but the payoff for all the exertion is both palpable and provable. In 2000, Stern Stewart published its second study that compared the stock market performance of EVA companies with that of their peer groups. Sixty-five companies that had implemented EVA were tracked for five years, as were their peers. The performance measure was total shareholder returns. The findings: "On average, investments in the shares of these [EVA] companies produced 49 percent more wealth after five years than equal investments in the shares of competitors with similar market capitalization." Overall, that additional wealth came to $116 billion.

The incentive to join the EVA flock is clear enough, but the commitment must be wholehearted. With top management enthusiastically pushing the program, training the troops in the rationale and mechanisms of EVA, and motivating them with achievable rewards, success is not assured—nothing is certain in this world—but it is within realistic reach.

Epilogue

EVA and the "New Economy"

GREGORY V. MILANO

The business world is changing at a pace we have not seen for many years. The expansion of the Internet and the advance of telecommunication technologies are offering many new channels for media distribution and communication. Many observers view this as a completely new paradigm for business where the rules of the game are changing. New market entrants are breaking into established markets at a pace most of us could not have anticipated. The dynamic of these "new economy" businesses is new in that there are more clicks and fewer bricks. Talented human capital is flowing into these businesses, making it difficult for traditional businesses to attract and retain the people they need. The new era is heralded as *the knowledge revolution*, following behind the industrial revolution and the information revolution. It is all quite exciting and challenging.

Unfortunately, some have naively commented that this means the end of EVA. They claim EVA is useful for old world companies with heavy investments in fixed assets, but they say the need to worry about capital charges is no longer an imperative. We strongly disagree. We have found that not only is EVA suitable for the emerging companies that lead the new economy, but EVA is even more important for these companies than it was for their older "rust belt" relatives. There may be a "new economy" with products and services available in revolutionary ways, but there are no "new economics." The principles of economic valuation remain the same, and EVA is uniquely suited to bringing a modicum of sense to new economy valuation.

The critics remark that because these newcomers have little or no current "profits," a dearth of hard assets, and an overhang of management share options, how could we possibly use financial statements to attribute real value to them? Pointing to the lack of buildings, machinery, and working capital, they say there is no need to consider capital investment levels.

The valuations have indeed hit lofty peaks at times. As of the end of the last millennium, Yahoo! was worth $110 billion, or over 20 percent more than Motorola, nearly 40 percent more than Morgan Stanley Dean Witter, and nearly 1,000 percent more than Textron! Unless we believe investors have totally lost their minds, there must be a plausible explanation.

Some say that these companies will generate enormous cash flow in the future. As discussed earlier in this book, the basic premise of modern corporate finance is that value is the sum of the present values of all future free cash flows a business is expected to generate. An investor need only forecast his or her expectations for the future revenue, costs, and capital; convert each year to a free cash flow figure; and calculate the present value. Simple, right? What's the Yahoo! cash flow forecast for 2014? What is the terminal value (i.e., the assumed value at the end of the explicit forecast)? With the cash flow approach applied to a business with such an unknowable expected future, we find the really important numbers are almost impossible to forecast. Discounted cash flow is theoretically correct but practically useless for the new economy.

We find it is much more straightforward to use the EVA approach. The benefit of EVA for "new economy" valuation is that it shows how a greater percentage of the value appears in the earlier years, when forecasting is more practical. Our studies show that, in a typical ten-year discounted cash flow analysis for a new economy company, 80 to 99 percent of the value is the terminal value. When we apply EVA with the same forecast, only 20 to 50 percent of the value is the terminal value. This helps give valuation experts more comfort with their answers and enables them to test the sensitivity of their assumptions in the crucial early years.

But the benefit of EVA goes beyond this by correctly treating as capital those cash outlays that represent investments as opposed to current expenses. It allows us to see the pattern of value creation, not just the present value. In our forecast, what is the year-by-year contribution to value? Cash flow just doesn't tell us. Many new economy companies are investing heavily to grow, and the resulting negative cash flow doesn't tell us much about performance each year. EVA, on the other hand, tells us how much contribution there is each year. Does the profit this year justify the cumulative investment—including soft investments such as product development and brand advertising—that we have made thus far? Security analysts and investors have an easier time checking that their forecasts make sense.

How does this help us to understand the value of new economy stocks? Most of these companies do not even have profits, let alone enough to cover a capital charge! Of what use is EVA?

Here we see a shortfall of accounting, not of EVA. The capital in a new economy company consists of research, development, marketing, advertising, and start-up costs. The accountants, apparently assuming that all the value is expected to materialize in the year the R&D money is spent, view these as expenses against current profits. As this book has argued, it is more realistic to capitalize these investments and amortize them over their expected useful life, as EVA does. In fact, the entire accounting framework is more useless for these companies than for "old economy" companies.

It is easier to see the point with an actual example. RealNetworks, Inc. is a successful developer of software for displaying audio and video media on PCs and over the Internet. In looking at the 1995 through 1998 accounting statements for RealNetworks, Inc., we produced Table E.1. Over this period, RealNetworks incurred costs that were 35 percent higher than the revenue received. This leads critics to point out how useless accounting statements are for valuing new economy companies.

On closer examination, Table E.1 provides striking evidence of the negative bias that accounting accords research, development, selling, and marketing costs, which harms the perception of operating profit for a new economy company. For RealNetworks, these expenditures amount to 72 percent of total accounting expenses over this four-year period. How are investors supposed to use this information to understand performance? Even worse, if a company paid

Table E.1   RealNetworks, Inc., 1995–1998 Accounting Figures

| | Thousands of US$ | | | |
	1995	1996	1997	1998
Revenue	1,812	14,012	32,720	64,839
Cost of Sales	62	2,185	6,465	12,390
Gross Profit	**1,750**	**11,827**	**26,255**	**52,449**
General & Administrative	747	3,491	6,024	9,841
Selling, Marketing, & Advertising	1,218	7,540	20,124	32,451
Research & Development	1,380	4,812	13,268	29,401
Goodwill Amortization	0	0	0	1,596
Net Operating Profit	**−1,595**	**−4,016**	**−13,161**	**−20,840**
Percent of Sales	−88%	−29%	−40%	−32%

bonuses to generate operating profit, executives would be motivated to cut the very research, development, selling, and marketing costs that are driving the success of the company. Treating these expenditures as period expenses is like charging the cost of a chemical plant against operating profit in the year the plant is built. It is pretty senseless.

Despite the horrible accounting earnings trend, RealNetworks, Inc. has had stellar share price performance since flotation (see Figure E.1).

EVA does a better job of tracking the value of this business. When we adjusted the accounting statements to treat research, development, selling, and marketing as investments with a five-year life, we produced Table E.2.

We have always known that accounting standards do not provide very useful information to investors. With new economy companies, this is truer than ever. It has made exciting and paradoxical

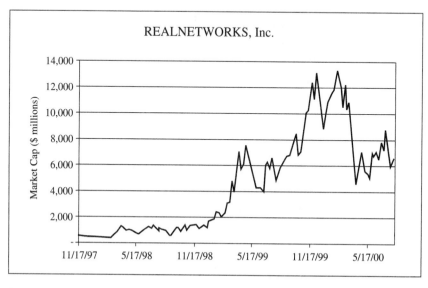

Figure E.1 **Share Price Performance, November 1997–May 2000**

Table E.2   RealNetworks, Inc., 1995–1998 EVA Figures

Economic Figures	Thousands of US$			
	1995	1996	1997	1998
Gross Profit	**1,750**	**11,827**	**26,255**	**52,449**
General & Administrative	747	3,491	6,024	9,841
Amortization of Cap. SM&A	154	1,074	3,529	7,488
Amortization of Cap. R&D	193	780	2,399	5,986
Net Operating Profit	**656**	**6,482**	**14,303**	**29,134**
EVA	**639**	**6,336**	**12,672**	**25,797**
Percent of Sales	35%	45%	39%	40%

journalism to continue speaking of companies with high valuations and no earnings, but this is just the result of an accounting
framework that is systematically flawed. Investors and managers
tracking performance of these companies should use EVA and
should treat expenditures in research, development, selling, and
marketing as investments, not period expenses. Even without going
through an EVA exercise, many investors behave in a way that indicates they implicitly make the same assumptions about R&D

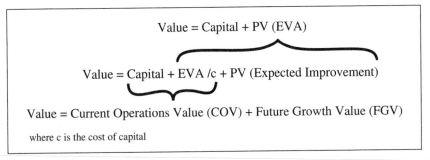

Value = Capital + PV (EVA)

Value = Capital + EVA /c + PV (Expected Improvement)

Value = Current Operations Value (COV) + Future Growth Value (FGV)

where c is the cost of capital

Figure E.2   Current Operations Value and Future Growth Value

and other long-term investments. EVA for RealNetworks, Inc. is, in fact, quite strong. It averaged 40 percent of revenue for the four-year period and rose to 44 percent in 1999. There do not seem to be many Old World companies that can deliver EVA after capital charges of this magnitude.

To dig deeper into the matter, value is driven both by performance today and by developing the core competency and competitive position to deliver value in the future. We can see this if we further develop our EVA valuation equation into two components, as shown in Figure E.2. The first is simply the present value of EVA if we assume the current EVA is repeated forever. This is calculated as the current EVA divided by the cost of capital. When this is added to the capital base, we see what the company would be worth if the market thought current performance would perpetuate. We call this the Current Operations Value (COV). The second is the present value of expected improvements in EVA from this point forward. We call this the Future Growth Value (FGV).

Where the FGV is a substantial percentage of the total enterprise value of a company, we should consider the components of FGV. Despite the strong EVA trends, virtually all new economy companies have the majority of current value in FGV.

There are three primary sources of FGV:

1. The expected growth in performance from currently marketed products.
2. The expected contribution of products in development that are just being released.
3. The benefit of products that the company has not even identified yet—the value investors are willing to assign to a company to recognize that there is some probability that a successful team will still come up with new ideas far out into the future. This is easily seen when considering a pharmaceutical company with currently marketed drugs, a pipeline of

hopeful compounds, and the know-how to develop new products into the future. The new economy is no different.

What is different for new economy companies is how high FGV is as a percentage of total market value. Here are four factors that drive FGV so high in these companies, despite a modest COV.

1. EVA Margin. Successful new economy companies have a very high EVA margin, and those that do not will often exhibit the potential to generate a very high EVA margin in the future. A much higher percentage of each dollar of revenue drops to the bottom line as EVA after all taxes and capital charges. In the case of RealNetworks, discussed above, this figure is about 40 percent. In 1998, it was 24 percent for AOL, 30 percent for Cisco, 44 percent for Microsoft, 17 percent for Oracle, and an amazing 59 percent for Yahoo! These figures are truly startling by Old World standards. Large players in the very successful pharmaceutical sector average EVA to sales below 10 percent. The new economy EVA margins are outstanding, largely due to an obliteration of variable costs, which often run less than 15 percent of sales. Tasks that were once completed by people are now completed by software. As Professor Paul Romer of Stanford University puts it, we are codifying recipes for activities that allow global scalability without people in the loop. He says we are converting wetware, or the knowledge in our heads, to software that can be replicated with near-zero costs. On top of this, there is very little traditional capital required in terms of bricks and mortar. Taxes, too, are kept very low since all the investments in research, development, marketing, and advertising are written off in the year incurred. As Peter Keen said at the EVA Institute Senior Management Conference in March 2000 in Florida, "[The] key factor to monitor is the marketing cost to acquire customers, and then the growth in repeat business, and the repeat business per transaction. Now once you have the repeat business, then you can move to digital margins. And digital margins average about 80 percent." These very high EVA margins make every dollar of current volume and future sales growth several times more valuable than comparable Old World companies.

2. High Growth Rate. Most of these companies are quite small, but are growing very rapidly. Although growth for growth's sake is not very value-creating, when this is coupled with very high EVA margins; the value implications are enormous. Many new economy companies have networks that foster growth since the value to each successive customer grows as the size of the network grows. In his book, *New Rules for the New Economy*, Kevin Kelly wrote: "The first fax machines cost several thousands of dollars and connected to only a few machines, and thus were not worth much. Today, $200 will buy you a fax network worth $6 billion." For successful new economy companies, this fosters amazing growth. By 1998, RealNetworks had a three-year compound annual growth rate of 230 percent per year. For AOL, the figure was 99 percent, for Cisco 62 percent, for Microsoft 35 percent, for Oracle 34 percent, and for Yahoo! another amazing result at 430 percent. These figures appear to be unsustainable and usually decline as the company grows, but the point is that a fast growing, very profitable business can be worth much more than its relatively stagnant Old World counterpart. It is no wonder Yahoo! has the valuation that it does. For the major players in the pharmaceutical sector, the average growth during this period was about 11 percent.

3. Low Current Market Share. Although current growth rates are important, it is the potential for future growth that influences the forward forecasts of investors. Growth can come from an expansion of the market category or from stealing market share from others. The new economy, by its very nature, has served to expand certain markets for products and services. There are new channels for purchase; for example, a book sale by Amazon.com does not nec-essarily mean a bookstore missed a sale. Many of these sales would not have occurred if the new channel were not available. However, a large percentage of long-term growth comes from pilfering market share from others. Thus, an important indicator of how long the growth can last is the present market share represented by the com-pany. As long as this is a small percentage, there is plenty of room for growth by encouraging customers to switch.

4. Ability to Differentiate. In the new economy, barriers to entry are often quite weak. Just as the current Internet stars invaded the turf of entrenched players, new upstarts can invade their turf. Further, customers can readily comparison-shop on price, leading to intense price pressure. As Lord Kenneth Baker said, at the EVA In-stitute Senior Management Conference in September 1999 in France, "Distribution margins will be under immense pressure. This is what the Internet does more than anything else. If goods can be sold as easily as this, they will incur fewer costs. The balance has shifted to the consumer." This is true, unless the new economy firm can readily differentiate its products from those of competitors. Products or services that are differentiated establish barriers to entry and price protection. The value of a business is much higher if it can sustain margins and growth rates for the long term, and this is essential to high-value figures.

Essentially, the first two drivers of FGV—EVA margin and sales growth—are what make a company valuable. The third driver, low current market share, allows the sales growth to be extendable out into the future, and the final driver, differentiation, fortifies the EVA margins to be more robust over time.

To see the strong impact that EVA margins and sales growth have on value, we consider two hypothetical companies. The first is a sound performing Old World Company (OWC) and the other is a rising upstart New World Company (NWC). OWC has $2 billion in annual sales with $1 billion in invested capital. Its current EVA is $20 million, a 1 percent EVA margin. The company is growing at 5 percent per year and is expected to continue this growth in the future while maintaining its EVA margins. With a 25-year time horizon and a flat EVA in perpetuity thereafter, the company has a present value of $1.33 billion. This company is considered a solid, if not exciting, performer because its market value exceeds book value by only 33 percent.

The second company, NWC, is very small but growing fast. Sales are now only $10 million on $5 million in capital, including capitalized R&D and marketing. EVA is now $3 million, a 30 percent EVA margin. NWC generated growth of 100 percent this past year, and the surplus growth over 5 percent is expected to decline by 10 percent per year. In other words, growth is expected to be: this year, 90.5 percent; next year, 82.0 percent; and so forth. The EVA margin is also expected to decline in a similar manner. Even though this company is only 5 percent of the size of OWC, the current total market value is exactly the same: $1.33 billion. The market value exceeds book value by thousands of percent.

This yields a valuation for NWC that is 133 times the present level of sales. As the company grows, this multiple will undoubtedly come down, but it is still a staggering number to consider. When we look back at Yahoo! in 1998, with an EVA margin of 59 percent (twice the level of NWC) and three-year trailing compound annual growth rate of 430 percent (over four times NWC), perhaps a valuation over $100 billion at the end of 1999 is not too far out of reach. This valuation was about 500 times 1998 sales.

The power of growth and EVA margins is thus illustrated. It will take 17 years, given these assumptions, for NWC to grow to be larger in sales than OWC. But the value in present terms is still the same.

We should bear in mind that the COV of OWC is nearly 90 percent of the total market value, while the COV for NWC is a mere 2.2 percent of value. With so much of the value of NWC based on the future, we would expect the share price to be much more volatile as the market constantly readjusts the expectations for the future. In essence, this is why we see so much stronger rises and falls in the NASDAQ, a market heavily influenced by the new economy, than we do in the Dow Jones Industrial Average. Much more of the value of the NASDAQ is dependent on the future and therefore subject to frequent revision.

When a considerable amount of a company's value is in FGV and that future value is quite variable, a better understanding of intrinsic value may be gained by applying "real options" techniques as suggested earlier in Chapter 11. This is almost becoming a cliché in financial circles, but our experience is that a minority of those who talk about option techniques truly understand their relevance or practical use in valuation. The analysis can be somewhat more complex than applications to oil and gas, where enormous databases on price and cost trends are available, but the technique is helpful nonetheless.

On January 30, 2000, Barry Riley wrote, in *Financial Times*, "The S&P 500 returned 21% last year but the median stock returned zero, which is another way of saying that 250 stocks lost you money. You had to be in technology." Although this sounds startling, it is not an uncommon outcome. We usually see a small percentage of shares that do so well that they pull up the average to a point well above the median. In the familiar phrase, an option on a share gives the right, but not the obligation, to purchase and allows us to participate in this potential upside while avoiding the downside. The elimination of all these potentially negative outcomes causes the option value to always be above the in-the-money value.

As discussed in Chapter 11, several factors drive the value of options, but the single most important factor is the volatility of the asset value. In fact, the high degree of uncertainty about the future, and the many options available to new economy companies now and in the future cause their value to rise dramatically. These companies have so much of their expected performance ahead of them that their shares are, in essence, options on participation in the future.

To consider the impact of volatility on the value of options, we consider financial call options on two well-known companies: General Electric and Amazon.com. General Electric has a volatility of about 30 percent, and Amazon.com is about 100 percent. Using the standard Black–Scholes–Merton model for option valuation, we considered similar options on these two shares. With low volatility, the option value for General Electric drops away rapidly as the exercise price increases. But with high volatility, the option value for Amazon.com holds quite high, even at very high exercise prices. Indeed, with a standardized share price of $10, a volatility of 100 percent, and an exercise price of $30 (three times the current price), the option in Amazon.com is still worth $6.23, or 62.3 percent of the share price. And this is with a time frame of five years, which is long for a financial option but short for the real options faced by new economy companies. By contrast, a similar option with an exercise price of $30 on General Electric would be worth $0.572. So an option to buy Amazon.com at three times the current share price over the next five years would be worth nearly 11 times (6.232/0.572) that of a similar option to buy General Electric. This, again, is due to the importance of the tremendous upside on highly volatile shares.

The key point is that a financial option gives the holder the privilege without the requirement to purchase a share for a specified price over a specified time. It can be worth substantially more than we might think. The greater the volatility and uncertainty, the more valuable the option becomes. But the benefit of this valuation approach extends far beyond mere financial options. Every operating decision that a company faces provides options, which can be quite valuable, particularly in times of great uncertainty. To understand new economy valuation, we must understand the value of real options.

Companies of all types are faced with real options every day. In start-up companies where much of the potential income of key employees is in the form of stock options, the cost of the human capital essentially involves optionality. If the company does well, the human capital reaps large rewards, but it gets nothing if the company doesn't do well. The fact that the providers of human capital absorb some of the downside potential is a source of option value to the shareholders.

The future of the new economy provides more options than ever before. If a company is positioned with substantial content and a large subscriber base, it stands to make significant gains when there is an increase in bandwidth to households. Advanced telecommunications, video telephones, movies-on-demand, work-from-home capabilities, and a whole host of other potential future developments become possible. When this happens, there will be investments in infrastructure to handle the throughput, but these investments will only be made when the technology makes them valuable.

Companies such as AOL and Yahoo! are positioning themselves to take advantage of the increased future potential by establishing the right, not the obligation, to invest in these areas. Significant option value results. Every company in every industry has such strategic options, and this adds value to their shares. But, as we saw above with financial options, the value of out-of-the-money options (those that cannot yet be exercised for any proceeds) is much higher when volatility and uncertainty are high.

If we think of the entire extended sector as one valuation problem, we can picture a portfolio of available options. The collective value of these options, when combined with the value of current activities, is the sum of the total value of all companies in the extended sector. The judgment managers need to make is: which options are most valuable? To do this, managers have to look at the drivers of value.

Let's consider a simple example of a single real option. In the banking and brokerage business, there is a strong move toward on-line transactions, but the reality is that only a small percentage of clients have signed up for this service. And even these people still mix on-line banking with telephone and face-to-face banking. The investments the banks are making in this field may not be earning an adequate return right now, but the banks have purchased an option to participate in this new customer service.

Will it ever be the case that the vast majority of all banking, both commercial and private, will take place over the network? Will Peter Keen ever be right when he says, "The world needs banking but it probably does not need banks"? We do not know. There are technological and cultural barriers to rapid acceptance. Most people do not have computers at home, and they are being discouraged from surfing the Internet for personal use at work. However, it may be that the marginal cost reduction, fixed asset reduction, improved consistency of service, and overall convenience will draw people in quite rapidly.

If the transition does occur, it could be worth hundreds of billions of dollars in value, some of which will be transferred to consumers. The banks will retain the rest. If it passes by with little acceptance, it's worth nothing, but the companies will also have avoided the larger investments in infrastructure. Thus, they have purchased the right, but not the obligation, to grow an Internet banking service.

If we return to thinking about the extended new economy sector, then go on to consider who will win and who will lose, we have an easier time grasping the issues. Who would have guessed, in 1980, that Microsoft would replace IBM as the powerhouse of computers? But we all could have predicted that the use of computers would rise and someone would make a lot of money. Too many commentators waste too much effort discussing whether AOL will win, or Amazon, or eBay. Before we even consider the relative slice of the pie, and the high variability in this, we should consider the size of the pie, which itself has a very wide range of possible outcomes.

The new economy sector, as it should be considered, is really made up of several sectors in the traditional sense. We start with the dot-com companies. But these would be of little interest without content, so we must consider companies that own content. These are the media companies such as Time Warner and Disney, but the group includes any company that owns content of interest to people or businesses, such as maps, census data, and encyclopedias. Next, we consider appliances, which is the new word for any piece of e-equipment such as computers, televisions, phones, and a wide range of focused application appliances beginning to come to market now. This sector includes not only equipment providers such as Dell and Sony, but also important suppliers to them, such as Intel. Then people need platforms such as search engines and operating systems to be able to use their appliances, so companies such as Microsoft and Yahoo! fit in. Finally, we need a means of communication, so the telecommunications companies—including telephone, wireless, and cable providers—are included.

The importance of considering the extended sector comes in two forms. First, innovations in one subsector can transform all the other sectors immediately. If the telecommunications folks figure out how to get ten times the volume down the copper wires connected to most houses, this allows more elaborate Web sites with lots of video and user-friendly features. Content such as high-quality video, which is now nearly unavailable on the Web, will suddenly be readily accessible. The state-of-the-art for dot-coms goes up to the benefit of content providers, and this requires new appliances and platforms. The frequency of innovation in this group of subsectors is remarkably rapid.

When we consider the extended sector as a whole, we see some companies with different mixes of value contribution over time.

We break these into two groups. There are those that are creating a lot of value now. Others are creating very little value now but have enormous value attributed to them in the future. The latter cause most concern about the reality of valuations. The collective group can be thought of much as we view a pharmaceutical port-folio. A pharmaceutical company has a group of drugs it now markets. Typically, they produce very high current value and may have some opportunity for growth. They also have a pipeline of com-pounds which drain resources now but are expected to create sub-stantial value in the future.

Investors accept that the pipeline of a pharmaceutical company contributes significantly to the current valuation of the company, even though these compounds are running losses and draining re-sources every year, and do not promise the chance of profit contri-bution for many years. Yet many of these same people are unwilling to accept that a new economy stock with similar economic charac-teristics may contribute considerable value as well. The dynamics are the same, except the pharmaceutical compound is being man-aged inside a company that is also producing products and deliver-ing profits now. The new economy stock is out on its own.

Another component of pharmaceutical valuation should be con-sidered. It is generally estimated that 15 to 40 percent of the value of a pharmaceutical company comes from the long-term future—com-pounds that are not yet in the development pipeline and may not even have been discovered by researchers. In other words, the market is willing to recognize that, although we do not know what they will be working on in the future, it is likely to deliver value.

The value of the "unidentified future" plays an important role in the value of pharmaceutical companies. This applies to the ex-tended new economy sector as well. Due to patent lives, future value must come from new compounds in pharmaceutical companies, but new economy companies have no definitive life dictated by a patent so they can have future value beyond the life of current products. Of course, some of the future value will come from companies that are now emerging or may not have even formed yet.

If we take the extended new economy sector as a whole, we see a valuation problem that is very similar to valuing a pharmaceutical company. The difference is that, in pharmaceuticals, we have many integrated companies that perform research, development, production, and marketing. They own currently marketed drugs, a pipeline of potential drugs, and the know-how to create new drugs in the future. In the new economy, we have integrated companies, but we also have numerous "pipeline" companies that operate separately.

People often ask whether the new economy shares are priced too high or too low. From a trader's perspective, this is obviously a critical issue. During 2000, the NASDAQ ranged up and down from 3,000 to 5,000 and individual shares swung even more. It is tough to time purchase and sell orders in this environment. But this book really is not aimed at traders, but at executives and long-term owners—those who want to create real long-term value. From this perspective, the up-and-down swings in the market are interesting, but underlying value creation is what matters. It is important to develop, for the new economy, a strategy that produces underlying value.

Despite all the hype, much of the strategic thinking behind success in the new economy mirrors the factors of success in the old economy. That is, value is created when we deliver a product or service that is desired by customers and distinguished from competitors so that the price of the product or service is well above the total cost, including the cost of capital, for delivery. As discussed previously, this is achieved by adoption of an appropriate value discipline and superior execution of strategies and tactics.

Why, then, was Amazon.com worth $26 billion while Barnes & Noble was worth $1.4 billion at the end of 1999? What are the strategy implications for an Old World company that is trying to survive in the new e-world?

Oddly, the biggest change is time. The new economy simultaneously shrinks and lengthens time horizons. Technology shrinks time due to the rapid rate of development. We need to constantly adapt our service offering to new media, new platforms, and new access. The benefits come from the network and the interconnection we all now have. Combining this with the ever-increasing speed with which we can transmit immense quantities of bits and bytes gives a linked interface we have never before experienced.

How should managers react? Whether old or new, rapidly take full advantage of the Web. This sounds straightforward, but many old economy management teams view their business as being separate or insulated from new technology. "Sure, there are Internet companies that compete with traditional retailers, but I make windows, so what does it mean for me? It's just a waste of money!" It is easy to fall into this trap, but the Web is not really about retail trade, though this is perhaps the most advanced. It is about connectivity. Every business will benefit from better connectivity whether it links to customers, suppliers, employees, whatever. Each company should use this advance to create new value and develop a competitive advantage.

And it is not enough to have a Web site. As *The Economist* wrote on June 26, 1999, these are often "stodgily designed billboards, known in the business as 'brochure-ware,' which do little more than provide customers and suppliers with fairly basic information about the company and its products." This is not really using the Web; there needs to be interaction, transaction, and just plain action.

The new economy also lengthens time frames in that investors are satisfied to wait for results as never before. One of the biggest obstacles for large companies is that their time horizon and excessive focus on quarterly or yearly earnings make it hard for them to be as patient as they should be. This is not a Wall Street problem. It is a management fixation.

Be more patient with Internet investments. If you are pursuing the right strategy and getting the right results, even if this means sacrificing near-term accounting earnings, investors will understand, but only if management carefully explains the nature of what it is doing and why. In fact, investors will likely compliment you. In this process, we must avoid the temptation to say that companies that cannot produce accounting earnings have no profits. Use a better system of measurement where investments in soft assets are treated on a level playing field with investments in hard assets, and all investments are required to generate a return over time.

Ignore accounting statements; treat research, development, selling, and marketing costs as investments; and measure business performance with EVA. The antiquated system of accounting that is prevalent in all countries discourages managers from making the right Internet decisions. Just say no! Silicon Valley in California, and all the regions of the world that operate the same way, has evolved into a perfect technology greenhouse. It is a Development Director's dream with small sums of money directed without bureaucracy toward lean organizations with energized teams and great ideas. There is a tremendous ability to fund ideas, wait for them to mature, and shut them down if they fail. Although most of the investments fail, the winners can be blockbusters.

In too many Old World companies, this mechanism just would not work. The corporate staff analysts would develop statistics on how the majority of investments fail, and the CEO would use this analysis to berate the business manager. Business managers learn pretty quickly in most companies that minimizing failures is a lot more important than maximizing successes. And thus, the innovation potential of most Old World companies, particularly those that are large, is stifled.

Experiment and accept failure as integral to the learning process. Even outside Silicon Valley, Americans tend to be more tolerant of failure than Europeans. This is essential. If we knew in advance which new economy investments would fail, we would not make those investments. But we do not know, so we have to invest in a portfolio. As long as the successes earn an adequate return on the portfolio of investment, we are successful. And do not just tolerate failure, but ensure a disciplined learning process. Through experimentation, some of the best ideas for products and services are dramatic shifts in focus for the originating company.

Think, outside the box, about ways the interconnected world can help you deliver your product or service more efficiently, or make your offering more valuable and differentiated versus competitors'. Don't just think about selling through the Web; consider the greater value chain. Can you increase customer awareness, increase accuracy of orders through direct access, coordinate better with suppliers to avoid excessive inventory stocks, gather useful product development information, or allow more customized product design? Look at what others are doing in unrelated sectors, and brainstorm ways of applying their techniques. Do not think you have to do it yourself; you can partner with specialized companies that offer technology solutions. Use what the new economy offers to make your business more effective for your suppliers and customers, and you will be the preferred business partner.

However, avoid overinvestment in advance of commercial possibilities. The focus should be on making many small investments that create the ability to seize opportunities when they arise without being tied to technologies and activities that may not prevail. As stated previously, investments in joint ventures, strategic alliances, and the like can be an economically efficient way of participating in the potential of new technologies. To repeat: option value is created when we have the right, but not the obligation, to invest. Do not commit too early.

Invest in real options, and position your company to have as many valuable opportunities for the future as possible. In essence, we can say that option value comes from the flexibility we develop.

This can be in the form of flexibility to invest or disinvest when the time is right. None of us has a crystal ball. We have to do our best to position ourselves to win across a range of possible future scenarios.

The people we have managing our Internet activities will make or break our success. The tendency of large companies to be bogged down in bureaucracy will mitigate against success. Too often, managers are more concerned with looking good in the near term than they are with performing well. We have to make sure the interests of these managers are closely aligned with the performance we want them to generate.

Recognize the value of human capital, and allow the true stars to participate in the success of the organization. This can be accomplished through equity participation, or stock options, in the Internet business, but this will only work if the intention is to float the Internet activity separately. Do not feel compelled to float the new activity unless it is truly separate from the rest of your business. In many cases, the use of technology just adds sales or operational channels but is basically the same business. Growth in the business can often be accelerated by establishing a coordinated strategy where the traditional parts of the company help drive the new part. In retail, this is easy to see. Stores are motivated to encourage shoppers to move online, because they will still get credit if the shipping address is in their region. A separate floatation or tracker share should only be considered when there is no benefit to coordinating old and new.

Often, in the formative stages of development, when incentives are most important, it is far better to tie the rewards of management to an aggressive EVA bonus plan that encourages multiyear continuous improvement in performance (e.g., as is shown for RealNetworks above). The balance of risk and reward should typically be more highly leveraged than the average incentive plan, to provide adequate upside reward. The basic structure is the same as any EVA bonus plan. Key personnel will leave for the ever-growing number of Internet start-ups if they feel they do not have the opportunity to be adequately rewarded in their current positions.

Do not be distracted by the values of new economy companies. The share prices may be realistic or they may be a dream; we do not know. However, we do know that if we look at RealNetworks, its share price at the end of the 1999 financial year would have had to fall by 99 percent before it would have been worth less than the capital invested. At any reasonable percentage of prevailing valuations, this would be an NPV to capital ratio that many Old World companies would cherish. Given such high values, get out and do it.

Stop thinking about survival. Take an offensive position. Although the Old World companies tend to have more assets, more staff, and more history, they are considered the underdog in this New World. Everybody loves it when an underdog wins, but this will only happen if the Old World companies believe they can win and then lead the way. A big step is overcoming the fear of cannibalization. Too many companies refuse to make the hard choices that allow the transition, for fear of undercutting the old established guard. Just remember, if you do not cannibalize yourself, others will do it for you. If there is a better and more efficient way to do it, someone will figure it out.

In mid-1929, Professor Irving Fisher, a noted economist in his day, forecasted that share prices had reached a permanently high plateau. Over the next few years, the Dow Jones Industrial Average dropped disastrously. Right now, we do not know if we are in the same situation. Are the recent valuations a bubble? Maybe so, or maybe not. However, we do know that the changes we can expect are significant, and companies that ignore them might as well be producing buggy whips. Every chief executive must steer his or her company into this great unknown. Understanding the drivers of value in this sector is critical to success.

The future of EVA is looking quite strong as the new economy unfolds and the need to recognize a broader range of investments intensifies. The critical sources of value creation are no longer based on bricks and mortar, but on clicks, connectivity, and access. New economy companies have demonstrated EVA margins and growth rates that have never been seen in the traditional economy companies, a lure for every company to jump in. There is no magic formula for value. The very same microeconomic principles that have driven value in the past will drive value in the future. But the way these companies create value has changed, and the rate of change seems to be constantly accelerating. The time is *now* for companies to step away from their bureaucratic roots and energize their staff to be more imaginative, creative, and entrepreneurial. EVA is the tool that successful companies will use to transform their culture toward one of entrepreneurship and ownership, driving rapid innovation.

Acknowledgments

This project has been a work of joy, in part because of the collaboration and friendship that has developed among John Shiely, who has been a dear friend for more than a decade, Irwin Ross, our journalistic mentor, and ourselves. John is one of the heroes of the EVA revolution, primarily because he recognized earlier than almost anyone else in the business community how the conceptual foundation and the day-to-day methodology could make a real difference in motivating people in operations who knew little about financial statements or corporate finance. It is never easy being at the front of the queue. His questions, his perception, and his drive to make it work, served as an example to other firms and to Stern Stewart of the proper way to convert theory into practice.

Irwin Ross is one of the finest writers in the business community. His literary and intellectual interests have provided us with discussions about philosophy, psychology, and sociology, while dealing with the economics of information, informational asymmetries, and incentive signaling. As I have mentioned to him on many occasions, however, the subject of EVA originated in the classroom at the University of Chicago in the Graduate School of Business.

The first example was a meeting with Dean George Schultz (later to become the secretary of labor, the director of the Office of Management and Budget, the secretary of the Treasury in the Nixon administration, and the secretary of state in the Reagan administration), who encouraged me to cross-register in the economics department to explore microeconomics as the fundamental basis for all the subjects in the Graduate School of Business. Of course, he was correct. Reading the works of Professor Gary Becker helped me focus on the important issue of incentives in determining human behavior.

Milton Friedman provided the laboratory thinking that was necessary to push the intellectual aspects of our ideas no matter where they took us and Merton H. Miller was the most significant contributor to the basic ideas on what determines the value of the firm.

As I have told my students in classes at Columbia, Carnegie-Mellon, the University of Michigan, the University of Rochester, the London Business School, and the University of Witwatersrand in Johannesburg, it was not just the seminal paper by Franco Modigliani and Merton Miller in 1958 on cost capital and capital structure that was so important; but rather the paper published in October 1961 in the *Journal of Business* titled, "Dividend Policy, Growth, and the Valuation of Shares," Section 2, and footnote 15 in Section 3, which provided the bases for lengthy discussions with Professor Miller concerning what the market really capitalizes. It was he who convinced me to ask the right questions, such as, why intangible assets are written off immediately in the accounting framework, but provide long-term value in the economic model of the firm. His classes were among the most stimulating. Imagine classmates that included Marshall Blume, Michael Jensen, Richard Roll, and Myron Scholes. Each of these economists became my teachers without knowing it, either by listening to them in class discussions, or by reading their path-breaking papers over the next twenty-five years. Such was the environment at the University of Chicago and in Merton Miller's classes.

No doubt Michael Jensen played a greater roll in the formulation of the EVA practices and design structure because of his insights that began with his pioneering "agency theory" (coauthored with the late William Meckling), where we were warned that management could act in interests other than shareholders, and thus shareholders would need to impose upon themselves the costs of monitoring management behavior, especially employing compensation structures that more closely align management and shareholder interests. His paper on free cash flow in the mid-1980s certainly demonstrated the danger of hoarding surplus assets in the firm and the threat to shareholder interest should such assets be used to cross-subsidize poor returning projects. His *Harvard Business Review* paper in 1989, "Eclipse of the Public Corporation," caused considerable support and conflict at Stern Stewart. Several of our professional staff felt his observations were correct and served as a fundamental stimulus to my colleague's book, *The Quest for Value*, in which Bennett Stewart suggests using high-debt ratios, possibly down deep into the firm (perhaps even in phantom form), in order to extract value and to encourage minimum waste.

Others in the firm believed that Professor Jensen's concerns could be overcome by contractually obligating the firm in carefully designed incentive structures that would expunge the surplus to shareholders and would activate all employees, not just management, to become value-change agents. Firms in mature, smokestack industries that might have been given up for dead would prove under the latter format to be merely dormant and, with the proper EVA motivation and mind-set changes, truly tremendous value-enhancing energies would be released. These are the real stories at Briggs & Stratton, Herman Miller, and SPX, to mention only the most obvious.

I most certainly thank Brian Walker at Herman Miller, Inc., for his commitment and drive to make EVA work in his firm, where a Scanlon approach had been used and became quite popular. John Blystone, a true intellect from General Electric, rescued SPX, where EVA had yet to be implemented. Upon his arrival at SPX, John recognized the critical contribution EVA could make. And across national boundaries, success has come at Siemens in Munich, Tate & Lyle in London, Orkla in Oslo, Lafarge in Paris, each with chief executive officers and finance directors who recognize the sustainable and evolutionary contribution EVA makes to employee satisfaction as well as value maximization. We see the same in former state-owned enterprises that have been privatized and are busy creating unexpected shareholder value, including Telecom New Zealand, Telstra in Australia, Singapore Power, the Port Authority of Singapore, and the United States Postal Service.

John Shiely, Irwin Ross, and I are deeply in debt to the professionalism and creativity of my colleagues at Stern Stewart. We have an intellectually rich environment that questions existing approaches to the maximization of value. I recall the critical sessions in David Glassman's office and frequent discussions with Donald Chew, editor of Stern Stewart's *Journal of Applied Corporate Finance*. Donald has been instrumental in getting my ideas focused. Gregory Milano showed us how to bridge the cultural gap by introducing adjustments to the European theater. He alone was responsible for extending these ideas to Australia, New Zealand, and South Africa, where we watched David Sussman, chief executive of the J.D. Group, and Trevor C. Honeysett, chief executive of New Clicks Holdings, Ltd., in Cape Town and Priceline in Australia, more than triple their value in under three years. John McCormack, senior vice president of Stern Stewart and head of our energy practice, has provided remarkable insight into the development of the theory of real options, which is being explored with Mark Shinder, vice president, in the pharmaceutical industry. Al Ehrbar, senior vice president and author of *EVA: The Real Key to Creating Wealth* has always provided intellectual underpinnings and focus in the development of my ideas. We first met more than twenty-five years ago when he was writing for the Personal Investing section of *Fortune Magazine*. Every writer needs a close friend to explore new ideas, where the climate is likely to be the least vulnerable. Dennis Soter has been this friend to me. We have known one another for more than thirty years, but friendship almost always has preceded the intellectual jawboning, and for this I am deeply thankful.

Approximately six years ago, our good friend, Sir Ronald Trotter, retired chairman of Fletcher Challenge, Ltd., Auckland, New Zealand, was told that I had forgotten to renew my visitor's visa; and thus I would be unable to attend an important meeting with his firm. Sir Ronald's response was, "Oh, you won't need a visa. Just tell immigration that you are a missionary." Such zealousness was a lonely route for me after graduating from the University of Chicago in 1964. I attempted to convince others that the accounting framework needed fixing, so that intangible assets would appear on the balance sheet where they belonged, instead of being expensed all in the current year. Other items, such as operating leases, were recognized nowhere on the balance sheet.

In 1976, almost 25 years ago, I found my Joshua in Bennett Stewart. Ours has been a noble calling, where we have shared intimate feelings about the intellectual hurdles we faced and how best to proceed. Our ideas have overlapped so that our voices have appeared to be one, and with his remarkable capabilities, the road we have traveled has been a great joy. Almost all of my friends in the academic community silently wish that they could have been a part of this exciting journey. Bennett has always made certain that we studied every last question before proceeding to the next challenge. For this, I am deeply indebted to him.

Ultimately, this message offers thanks to teachers who have helped us see the light, focus our attention, and remind us that objectivity and the scientific method go a long way in differentiating ourselves. The true test is whether these ideas have survivability and evolve into insights developed by still others. This story would not be complete, however, without recognizing the important guidance and caring that have come from my parents, Boris and Irene Stern, whom I was moved to honor at the University of Chicago's Graduate School of Business, with an endowed chair. It is so rare that we ever have a chance to formally thank our most important teachers. To this, I am honored once again to add the name of my son, Erik, who has become one of my teachers, too. His focus on strategy and on circling the airport one more time to establish the clarity of arguments, is something I wish I had adopted even before he was born. His contributions have extended into the labor unions and the way they should think about EVA as well as how to reach out to governments in what appears to be culturally unfriendly territory, where socialism, statism, and regulation are the first words a child seems to learn after birth.

Checking the facts and avoiding embarrassment wherever possible, has been the special task of Tatiana Molina. She has made this project especially wonderful because of the warmth of her personality and her commitment to excellence, a rare combination. She has been meticulous and focused, with a smile like no other.

Finally, none of us ever stops learning and we hope that the readers of this volume will unhesitatingly provide us with their insights, so that we can continue to sharpen the arguments and improve the focus, and thus to enhance the likelihood of success in furthering the culture of EVA.

Joel M. Stern

We all know at least one. My earliest recollection of such a character was the guy in my freshman class at college who, within a few days of arriving on campus, had established relationships with the local carpet dealers to purchase carpet remnants for resale to students as "wall-to-wall carpeting" for our tiny dorm rooms. Other ventures in snacks and soft drinks would follow. While the rest of us were agonizing over Comparative Literature and Calculus 101, he was managing inventories and establishing distribution channels for his customers. But he, nonetheless, managed to earn decent grades.

Without yet having a course in cost accounting or microeconomics, he understood that cash was king; capital employed was to be managed down to the lowest level required to support the current business and projected growth. And he understood the importance of relationships in pulling this all off. So who are these people? They are, in simplest terms, *value creators:* The men and women who have the unique ability to put two and two together and get five. They are able to work the modern-day, commercial equivalent of the miracle of the loaves and fishes. And they perform a critical and virtuous role in society, as no prosperous community exists without them. Some are entrepreneurs, and some buy failing businesses and turn them around. Some operate one-man shows, and some function effectively in large corporations. Some are on mahogany row, and some are on the shop floor.

When Joel Stern first suggested that we collaborate on a book that would not only address the academic foundation for, but the practical challenges of, creating value in an organization, I was intrigued. I have always been fascinated, not only with the black art that is the value-creation process, but with the unique characteristics of the great value creators. Particularly impressive to me are the people like Sam Walton and Herb Kelleher, who have been able to create enormous amounts of value in industries like retail and air transportation, long identified as being inhospitable to value creation.

What is this alchemy? Can you identify the unique characteristics of value creators? Can anyone be taught this discipline or is it purely genetic? Can you institutionalize it in your organization so that it survives the death or retirement of the original Obiwan Kenobi of value creation? And finally, can you incentivize people in order to reward value-creating behavior?

As a young staff tax accountant serving on the compensation team in the Milwaukee office of Arthur Andersen in the late 1970s, I was vaguely uncomfortable with the things corporations were paying their top executives to do. While responding to incentives to grow revenues, increase earnings per share, or reduce identified costs, many of these executives were managing their companies into value oblivion.

It's about that time that some pioneering disciples of Nobel prize-winning economist Merton Miller attempted to develop metrics that would have practical applications in the measurement of value creation. After all, it's impossible to analyze anything you can't measure. My earliest influence was Al Rappaport of the Kellogg Graduate School of Management, who wrote a seminal piece on "Selecting Strategies That Create Shareholder Value" in a *Harvard Business Review* (May–June, 1981) article. This was followed in 1986 with his definitive book *Creating Shareholder Value*. Al's work was a big influence on my decision to pursue an MBA at the Kellogg School.

While Rappaport's concept was right on the money, I later became attracted to the work of Joel Stern and Bennett Stewart. I believed their EVA concept showed great promise for practical applications in corporate value-creation programs. I was heavily influenced by Bennett's groundbreaking work *Quest for Value,* and had the distinct privilege of working with him as the lead Stern Stewart partner on our EVA implementation program at Briggs & Stratton.

My influences in the business community have been many and varied, each one having a particularly strong capability in some aspect of value creation: Harry Quadracci, founder and president of Quad/Graphics (value of leverage and integrative relationships with employees); Tracy O'Rourke, CEO of Varian and Ken Yontz, CEO of Sybron, both formerly of Rockwell Automation (restructuring for value); Jack Rogers, CEO of Equifax (growth with capital discipline); Jack Murray, CEO of Universal Foods (practical applications of EVA); attorney Tom Krukowski (employee relations); Stuart Agres, executive vice president of Young & Rubicam (marketing and brand development); Geoff Colvin and Shawn Tully of *Fortune* magazine (development and communication of the concept); Frank Krejci, CEO of Wisconsin Furniture (perseverance in the face of seemingly insurmountable obstacles), and the many insights of my colleagues at the EVA Institute.

I would like to acknowledge several influences in the fields of academe and public policy, who continuously confirm that the foundation for some of the best practice is in good theory: Michael Jensen of the Harvard Business School (corporate governance); Jerry Zimmerman and Jim Brickley at the Simon School of Business at the University of Rochester (economics of organizational architecture); Peter Drucker of the Claremont Graduate School (organizational vision and information systems); Keith Christensen of the Kellogg Graduate School of Management at Northwestern University (strategy); Russ Ackoff, emeritus professor at the Wharton School, University of Pennsylvania (organizational design); Herb Northrup, also emeritus professor at Wharton (labor economics); Jim Stoner and Frank Werner of the Fordham University Graduate School of Business Administration (quality and value creation); and Father Robert Sirico of the Acton Institute, Michael Joyce of the Bradley Foundation, Laura Nash of Boston University, and Charles Sykes, author and senior fellow of the Wisconsin Policy Research Institute (religious, political, and ethical implications of value creation).

Many thanks are due to my associates at Briggs & Stratton for their valuable contributions to the development of our EVA program: Bob Eldridge, Jim Brenn, Jim Wier, Harry Stratton, Sandy Preston, Paul Neylon, Dick Fotsch, Tom Savage, Todd Teske, Jerry Zitzer, Greg Socks, Gary Zingler, George Thompson, Michael Hamilton, Steve Rugg, Mike Schoen, Joe Wright, Ed Bednar, Dave DeBaets, Judy Whipple, Charlotte Caron (who prepared and edited my manuscript) and others, but most importantly to Fred Stratton, who consistently supported our efforts, and encouraged us to experiment with refinements.

I would like to express my appreciation to all the partners and staff at Stern Stewart who continually upgrade my understanding of the EVA concept, including Al Ehrbar, Dennis Soter, David Glass-man, Greg Milano, and Don Chew.

I am very grateful to Irwin Ross for his help in editing my por-tions of the manuscript and pulling the authors' insights together as a coherent work. I consider myself very fortunate to have been ex-posed to his considerable literary talent and deep knowledge and ex-perience in business writing.

And finally, my deepest gratitude goes to my coauthor, without whom this book would never have been produced. Some of the most intellectually stimulating moments in my life have been my discus-sions with Joel Stern, and I have enjoyed immensely our "tag team" seminars, most notably our presentations to the Fortune 500 CEO Forum in San Francisco, and the World Economic Development Congress in Washington, D.C. It is out of those events that our de-cision to write this book precipitated. Joel is a great friend and a giant in the field.

I dedicate this book to my wife Helen, and my children Michael, Erin, and Megan, who have provided the supportive environment without which I could never have completed my portions of the manuscript.

John S. Shiely

As the journalistic mentor, I have immensely enjoyed the intellec-tual stimulation of this collaboration. At times, I've had to play the role of doubting Thomas, in order to clarify the argument, but both my principals have been agreeably indulgent. In the process, I've ac-quired a bit of an education in finance, for which I am grateful. And, as Joel wrote, we've spent many pleasant hours talking about many other things.

I am grateful as well to Al Ehrbar, an old friend from the days I wrote for *Fortune*, of which he was an editor. Al introduced me to Stern Stewart and EVA several years ago and gave me a number of assignments to write about EVA companies in the *EVAngelist*, the publication of the EVA Institute. I am also indebted to Don Chew, who first suggested me for this project and whose insightful reading of the manuscript was a great help.

Several paragraphs in Chapter 8 on EVA and Acquisitions first appeared in an article by Joel Stern titled "Boardroom Controls Give Conglomerates a Boost," published in the October 3, 1999 issue of the *Sunday Times* of London, which granted permission to reprint (© Joel Stern/Times Newspapers Ltd, 3rd October 1999).

In addition, some passages in the book about the Centura National Banks, The Manitowoc Company, Herman Miller, Inc., and Tate & Lyle first appeared in my EVAngelist articles. In the case of The Manitowoc Company, Tom Leander updated my article and shared the by-line. The great bulk of material about EVA companies is new, the result of many hours of interviewing executives at all levels, as well as some shop-floor workers. I am beholden to them as well.

We are all grateful to Greg Milano for contributing the Epilogue, which introduces EVA into new terrain. Portions of his text originally appeared in "Internet Valuation: Why Are the Values so High," an article in *EVAluation*, Vol.2, Issue 1 (February 2000), a publication of Stern Stewart Europe. Greg wishes to thank Erik Stern, Tomas Fend, Nikolaus Piza, and Kal Vadasz for their contributions.

Irwin Ross

Index